THE
RELUCTANT HEALER

THE
RELUCTANT HEALER

David Elliott

Hawk Press

The Reluctant Healer
By David Elliott

Published by:
Hawk Press
2272 Colorado Blvd #1205
Los Angeles, CA 90041
http://www.thereluctanthealer.com/
(323)908-6058

Names have been changed to protect the identity of private parties.

Book Cover Design by Robert Aulicino, Front Cover Photo by Rassell Baer
Illustrations by Ann Faison
Charts by Kathy Greathouse
Edited by Geoff Fairbanks, Kathy Greathouse, and Cierra Trenery

Publisher's Cataloging-in-Publication
(Provided by Quality Books, Inc.)

    Elliott, David, 1958-
       The reluctant healer / David Elliott.
       p. cm.
       LCCN 2004105190
       ISBN 0-9753910-0-3

       1. Elliott, David. 2. Clairaudience--Case studies.
    3. Spiritual healing and spiritualism.
     I. Title.

    BF1338.A3 2004   133.8'5'092
                      QBI04-700243

"Open the Work"

*I dedicate this book to all of you on the path of Spirit.
Sooner or later it will find you.*

&

To Ruby, Elliott, Julie, and the Family of Light

TABLE OF CONTENTS

LIST OF FIGURES AND TABLES

LIST OF EXERCISES

CHAPTER ONE

INTRODUCING THE WORK

In writing a book like this, readers are entitled to an overview of where I am coming from: what ideas I embrace and also what I am not about.

My philosophy about healing and this work is based on my life experiences. It is not a religion, teaching, group, cult, or New Age idea. I look at it as an Old Age Universal approach to living life to the fullest. I have gathered information here and there, but primarily I have been guided by my intuition to create this philosophy. The truth in the information has resonated deeply in me. I have kept the material that works and the rest I have discarded. I suggest you do the same.

I am not a shaman or medicine man even though I love and respect Native American and other indigenous cultures' approach to Mother Earth. I am not a yogi or teacher of Eastern philosophies, although I utilize and respect many of these philosophies to live by. I accept the notions of reincarnation and karma, although they are not central to my healing, which is based in the here and now.

I could go on and on about what I am and what I am not to try to give you a better idea of who David Elliott is; however, why waste your time. My philosophy is simple:

- We are all one.

- Love is the greatest force in the universe.

- I accept a Higher Power. The name of the Higher Power does not matter. I use the name God, and I recognize many names connected to this source of energy such as Allah, Yahweh, Jehovah, Nature, Spirit, Light, Jesus, Buddha, Krishna, Great Spirit, etc. To me the name does not matter, the energy of the Higher Power does matter.

- We all have access to the power to heal ourselves.

- All of us are healers in some aspects of our lives, and as we accept this power, our abilities to heal and help others are greatly enhanced.

These are some of the spiritual principles I work with. I am not here to convert or recruit people to do anything except set themselves free. Once they are free their work with me is done. I do not need followers. I am interested in leaders going out and helping individuals heal, helping all to remember who they are, and that we are one.

Although you may not use the word "healer" to describe yourself, you and I are both healers. I lived most of my life before reluctantly, and joyously, giving in to the idea; reluctantly, because I had been intent on a career as an actor in Hollywood, and joyously, because of the incredible satisfaction it gives. So much happened on my personal journey that convinced me that I am, indeed, a healer. My intention in this book is to lead you on a path to your own role as a healer by sharing my experiences, my discoveries, and my thoughts. Another true purpose of the book is to help make Spirituality accessible to every person who "wants more," and to every person who does not know they "want more" yet. Spirit has an incessant way of creeping into your life ever so subtly, gradually gaining your attention, and the more attention you give it, the more space it will take up—in a good way, of course! I believe we are Spiritual beings distracted by a human condition.

On a day many years ago, my friend Ann asked about energy work. Her life changed dramatically that day and she has been on a healing mission with her life ever since. She went to a workshop with me in Sedona, Arizona, moved there, and worked as a Spiritual guide for tourists for several years. Ann's quest for Spirit has taken her on many journeys since I first helped connect her to energy.

To begin, I open my life to you—the story of my roots, my childhood, and my journey with the work of healing. The first chapter of the book covers my journey to heal myself and offers exercises to put your journey in perspective. In the second chapter, I describe the components involved in healing work, so you can begin to apply these principles to heal yourself and others. In the third chapter, I describe the various tools I use. Everything in life impacts the work of healing, so the rest of the book explores how I use healing to make sense of the world and live a deeper, richer, happier life.

If you approach this material with an open mind and heart, I promise that you will receive something much deeper and wider than just my personal experience.

For a long time I was guided to write this book; now that it is complete, I feel a huge relief and satisfaction. When I say I was "guided," that is exactly what happened. I have a gift known as Clairaudience, or "intuitive hearing," which means that I receive messages from an inner and/or outer voice. My gift lies in the throat chakra, one of the seven major energy centers in the body, and it affects what I say as well as what I hear.

I often say, "I heard a voice, and the voice said... " Many people hear "voices" and do not have positive experiences. The guiding voice that I hear is God-like. Centered, peaceful, wise, and grounded, it can also be quite persistent and has a well-developed sense of humor. It is a little unusual to live with an inborn voice like this but I have grown to accept it. This book is one of the outcomes.

Right now, that may be enough for you to say, "I don't hear a voice and therefore I'm not a healer," or, "I cannot do what he does." Have patience my friend—we all have gifts and talents. There is a reason why you are reading this book. Follow through and stay with it long enough to discover that reason.

If you are thinking, "I am not a healer. I have enough trouble taking care of myself. Why do I need to read this?" Then you probably do need to read this. In fact, you may need to read this more than the person who is already sold on it. As I said, we are all healers in one way or another.

Life demands a person to change, grow, and evolve; otherwise one's Spirit, mind, and body may shrivel and die. Now, you may not use all of the healing techniques described herein. You will find some useful in healing yourself, and some more appropriate for working with clients. I suggest that you start by healing yourself. You will find that healing is contagious and that it feels wonderful to be free from some of the illusions about life. Go ahead—give it a shot! Give yourself some hope that you can do, accomplish, heal, feel, love, live, and participate in life again (or for the first time).

The purpose of my book is not to convince you of anything; rather, it is to open you to your potential as a human being. Most of us can use healing in our lives, and there is always room for more happiness and joy. You will find questions and exercises at the end of some sections. When you do these exercises, you will experience the movement of energy and receive healing. I call this book a healer's handbook and I hope that you will use it as such. Refer to it frequently, keep it handy—use it as more than a onetime read.

I have learned that when I pursue healing in my life, it follows me out into the world. So, enjoy the journey. It has been a great ride for me, and I believe it will be for you, too.

WHERE AWARENESS GOES ENERGY FLOWS

I often refer to the statement, "Where awareness goes, energy flows." I heard my mentor, Tim Heath, say this statement more than once. These are powerful words, so let them sink in; they are a primary element in the book. Concentrate on your enlightenment, and concentrate with intention to face your fears. Concentrate with intention to choose love and to choose to let go and let God do the work. This is not about you, and it is definitely not about your ego. This is the primary relationship on the path to enlightenment—focusing on what you want to experience without the interference of the ego.

When something resonates or hits home, try to focus on it: review it, think about it, and feel it. See what block it hits against, and choose love to melt through it. Allow the magic of the hummingbird to bring sparkle, Light, and color to your life. Have courage! If you trust the process, you will experience alchemy: fear transmuted to love. Open your heart now and prepare the garden.

Enjoy the ride. I will see you on the other side, as I am now holding a space for you. Keep focused on the Light. We are all Light. We are all the same. Stay aligned to who you are. We have work to do within ourselves to bring this earth back to balance. Let us begin.

MY HISTORY

Now, I will tell you about my roots to give you a flavor of who I am. While reading my story, begin to connect to your own roots and family history. And rather than trying to figure it out in your head, try to feel the energy and connect to the truth about your lineage to your heart.

I am from a small Catholic farming community in western Kentucky called Fancy Farm, named for the neat family farms of the late 1800s. These farms are still "fancy" today. The community of Catholics originally emigrated from England—some with Lord Baltimore—to Maryland and then to Kentucky, where many of their descendants still reside. I am fond of this part of my history, which connects me to my heritage and my people.

Mine was a typical farm family in the 1950 and 1960s. Of five kids, I was the second oldest child, and the oldest boy. I come from a long line of farmers, so most of my early memories had to do with life on the farm. My dad farmed during the day and worked at the General Tire and Rubber Company at night, and Mom was a full-time housewife. My early childhood memories are pleasant: I spent most of my time with my grand-dad—we were buddies—riding in his GMC pickup and on his John Deere tractor.

When I was almost six, my eighteen-month-old brother, Jeffrey, died in a freak accident. He fell out of his high chair, hit his forehead on the counter, and died of a brain hemorrhage. This marked the end of innocence for me, and also for my family. I remember how hard it was on my mom, and what a sad, helpless feeling I had. A small child myself, I did not know what to do for her or for anyone else in my family. In all fairness, my parents did not know what to do either. They were both twenty-eight, and they still had four other children. There was little time to grieve.

Clearly, this was one of the most dramatic events of my childhood. I now realize that during this time, I made several decisions about love, loss, and life. I observed firsthand that life is not forever, and I also saw how loss could upset the delicate balance of love in a family. I did not feel good, nor did I feel safe. I wanted life back the way it was: I wanted my brother back, and I wanted my mother back. It was a lot for a sensitive, observant six-year-old to handle.

After that time, my life filled up with school and farmwork. I had little time to play, as there was always work to be done. We had acres and acres of land on which we grew row crops of corn, soy-beans, wheat, and tobacco. We also raised livestock—beef, pigs, and a few horses. We had good times and hard times. Farm life can be a test of endurance, especially for a young man, yet I got through it and came out the other side with a tremendous work ethic.

School was mostly the same, with plenty of hard work. Until the seventh grade, Catholic nuns educated me, and they gave me mixed reviews. I excelled when I connected with a teacher, but I was an average student when I did not connect with a teacher. I had a reputation among those who did not "get me" for being difficult, but I was well-liked by people who did "get me." Yet I must admit, the "difficult" reputation has followed me through most aspects of my life.

It is amazing what we do to be accepted and loved, and also what we resist doing when we are not. My granddad always accepted and loved me; we were best friends. My dad and I had a more strained relationship. I worked hard to earn my keep, but it never felt like enough for him. Our relationship was so intense and combative that he once pulled a shotgun on me when I was sixteen. Several years later, Dad admitted that he came very close to pulling the trigger. His side of the story is much different than mine, and truthfully, the details are unimportant now. I recount this event because it was the first time I remember hearing the "voice." It said, clearly, "Don't push him or he will kill you."

Overall, I was a good kid. Most of my conflicts were with Dad, although I had a few altercations with the law for partying, and I was kicked out of two basketball games for fighting. I was passionate about my space and safety, and stood up for myself when pushed.

Basketball was the highlight of high school. I was one of the stars on the Fancy Farm Golden Gophers basketball team. In my mind, we were like the team from the movie *Hoosiers*. We did well for a tiny school, although we did not have a Hollywood ending. I still love basketball, and I play whenever I get a chance.

When it came time for college, I knew I had to leave the farm, yet I was unsure about what to study. I partied considerably from age sixteen to twenty, including drinking, smoking pot, and experimenting with other drugs, and I also dated a lot of girls. Then, around the age of twenty, I slowed the partying and went on to get an MBA degree. All in all, I ended up doing well, in spite of starting college with no study habits.

As I reflect on those years, I realize I was watched over, guided, and protected, particularly during dangerous situations involving accidents, alcohol, and fast cars. For example, one night I was arrested on a DUI and taken to the county jail. I spent the night with five or six other detainees in a holding area.

When I woke up in the middle of the night to relieve myself, I blacked out, and the next thing I knew, I awoke on my back. An old black man looked down at me, shook his head and said, "Son, I think you oughtta quit drinkin'." He then vanished, and I never knew if he was real or not.

I believe the man was an angel telling me to wake up. That was the last time I drank enough alcohol to black out and that was the last time I was drunk on tequila. In fact, it was one of the last times I was drunk, period, and the last time that I saw the inside of a jail cell. I was twenty-two years old.

Shortly after, I visited Los Angeles with my great uncle, Bill Faulkner. While there, my cousins planted a seed in my head to stay in California and become an actor or a model—a new idea for me. However, I got a job in agribusiness selling hybrid vegetable seed, moved to Florida, and worked there for three years.

After I settled in Florida, the subject of acting and modeling came up again. One of the first people I met in Miami was a photographer, who wanted to shoot some photos of me to give to his friend, who was an agent. Sure enough, the agent wanted to represent me, and I began a sideline career as an actor and model. I caught the acting bug after doing some commercials, and became frustrated as I watched other actors open up and express themselves. Why couldn't I do that? I worked hard at this, and within a short time I was consumed with acting; in 1987, I moved to Los Angeles. I studied acting and read a lot of books, determined to learn about emotions and how to set them free. This led me to study psychology, personal growth, and Spirituality. Acting and personal growth possessed me—I was on a Spiritual path and did not even realize it.

Then out of the blue, people began coming to me, excitedly telling me that I was a healer. I thought they were crazy. Several of these New Age, tree hugging L.A. people had seen psychics. I thought I might need therapy, so I gave it a try with three different therapists over the course of about three years. Each of them patted me on the back and said, "You are one of the healthiest people I know. I will take your money if you want, but..."

MEETING THE MYSTIC HEALER

Finally in 1991, I said to God: "Please send me some help. I need to know what's happening to me." The next thing I knew, I was driving from Burbank to Palos Verdes to meet a mystic healer named Tim Heath, who my friend Alicia raved about—she had firewalked with him in Sedona, Arizona (not something I necessarily advocate unless you have a proper guide, such as Tim).

I was to meet him at 8:00 a.m. on a Saturday morning. I waited for about twenty minutes, making small talk with his friend Joan. She said that Tim was in the sauna and I should just keep waiting. Finally, a big, overweight man with red hair and a graying beard walked in. I thought to myself, "Damn it, Alicia! I'm going to give this guy $100, and he's a goddamn hippie!" Already, I was pissed and felt ripped off.

Tim poured himself some coffee and got a pack of cigarettes. He said, "Follow me," and I figured since I was already here, I might as well go ahead. We went outside and sat on some lawn chairs. Tim asked me where I had issues, and I said, "Definitely with my dad." He said, "You might have more with your mom."

He said the obvious stuff was with my dad. With my mom, it was more hidden and benign. I was ready to prove him wrong. He said, "Why don't you tell me about your last relationship." I told him her name was Donna. He then proceeded to describe Donna and our relationship so clearly that I understood it for the first time. Bam! He had me. I did not see it with Mom yet, but I did with Donna.

Tim said, "You're Clairaudient." I said, "Huh?" He said, "Clairaudient. You often know the answer to people's questions before they ask them. You can hear people's thoughts." He was right, but doesn't everyone do this to some degree?

He said, "Does it get real intense around relationships?" I said, "Yes, it does." I had known when Donna lied, where she had been, and usually what she had been thinking. It was crazy... or was it?

Tim laughed a hearty belly laugh that I later grew to appreciate. He said, "Come on inside. Let's do some other work now." He had me lay on a bed and he showed me how to do a two-stage breath called pranayama yoga, a rebirthing breath made popular in the 1970s. He had his assistant, Dennis, work deeply on my body, and it hurt. Tim orchestrated the session, guiding me into my experiences. Soon I was flying, laughing, crying, screaming; I was in and out of my body, covering many lifetimes and states of existence. What a ride! Most of the time, I felt like I was levitating.

It was an amazing experience! Tim performed a ceremony over me with spray, bursts of air, and some stimulating sounds. In my heightened state, my imagination went wild. I found out later that he was ironing shirts next to the bed. What I heard was an iron, sprays of starch, and shirts being fluffed. I realized the imagination is an extremely powerful healing tool. Tim gave me a lot of ideas that I use today in my healing work.

When he told me I was a healer, I rolled my eyes and told him that others have said the same thing. He said, "What they speak is true. I know you, brother. We came here on the mother ship together. It was named *The Solar Wind*. You were one of the commanders with me." I thought, "These New Agers are so weird." I think he heard me, and we both laughed.

I later learned that Tim genuinely meant what he said about a mother ship called *The Solar Wind*, either from a past lifetime we spent together or possibly in a future one. Do not let me scare you off here. I have always made fun of it, yet when I think of it now, I am not so quick to dismiss it because so many of the other things Tim said have come true.

I say anything is possible. Rather than being sarcastic about his weird statements, I just let them be and reserved judgment, keeping an open mind. I learned that the things I judge are those I couldn't allow myself to have or experience. This is a defense mechanism that comes from fear. When I block myself from experiencing things, it is the direct opposite of embracing them. Judgment becomes an act of pushing away and blocking receptivity.

I told Tim that I went through the biggest breakup of my life with Donna and was in a lot of pain. I moved into a new apartment after the breakup and had a repeated vision for several nights, startled awake by a being standing by my bedroom door, and silhouetted by an outdoor light. When this happened my heart stopped and I freaked out for several seconds; each of these experiences lasted for what seemed an eternity. When I was totally awake, with my eyes wide open, the being was physically manifested with the outline of a person's body. How can I describe a Spirit such as this? Was it energy beyond my known universe, a visitation by a Spirit being? When this happened, I knew my world had changed. Was it the breakup that drew this being in? Was it because of the pain in my heart?

When I told Tim about it, he said, "Let's talk to him and see why he's here. Let's invite the being in." He told me to think about the being, and sure enough, I felt a sensation. I got chills when I realized he was in my consciousness. Tim said, "Ask him his name," and told me to spell it, letter by letter, without time to think. I quickly spelled Ezekiel, and the being confirmed it was his name. The being came closer in my mind and psychic sense, and his image appeared to me in my mind. Tim said, "Ask him if he has a message or a gift for you." Ezekiel said, "Yes, I am here to usher you through this time, to protect, and watch over you."

Immediately, I felt better. I could see Ezekiel in my mind's eye and he looked like the hermit from a deck of tarot cards: long, white hair, a beard, gray-blue eyes, and a hooded robe. This experience with Ezekiel was very real, and it seemed that I knew his purpose. He was a temporary messenger or guide for me. Suddenly, I realized he had been appearing to me in physical form at other times. I had met an old hobo in Oklahoma a few weeks before, and also saw him on a mountain bike trail in the middle of Angeles Crest National Forest. I saw him one last time as he jogged on another mountain trail I was riding on. We went in opposite directions, and I remember seeing those gray-blue eyes.

Finally, I knew his name. "Isn't that a biblical name?" I asked Tim. "He is here to help usher me through *what* time?" As it turns out, this "time" was the complete change of my life and purpose. Although reluctant to see myself as a healer, I began to get it. Now, what was I supposed to do?

THE GIFT

Tim told me that with Clairaudience, it would be easy if I just trusted my gift and my guides. He said, "Listen and you will hear the truth. This is not about you, it is about something bigger."

I was unsure about the responsibility of such a gift. Tim said, "Just do the healing work, and it will open all the doors." "What doors?" I said. He replied, "The ones you want to walk through."

Tim also encouraged me to write, and he told me that I would write a book to help lift the consciousness of the planet from the second chakra—the love of power, sex, food, and money—to the fourth chakra, the heart, the power of love. "As a writer, you are not unlike John Lennon," he said. "Writing about humanity, helping lead people to the Light. You are a scientist on a frontier leading people to the Light." I liked the sound of that, yet I did not believe it was true. It just seemed like too much responsibility.

Tim told me that Clairaudience is a gift, even more rare than clairvoyance. He helped me clear the junk out of my chakras and out of my belief system, and he encouraged me to look at my fears, judgments, and my unwillingness to forgive. I was ready to grow and open up, and it felt great. I loved his work and really did not care about developing mine. I rode on his coattails for a while, observing him at work, still reluctant to do it myself. I set him up with people I knew, and he kept pushing me to develop my skills to do the work. Finally, when we were in the room with clients, he would leave. Sometimes he stayed away for what seemed a long time. It scared me and brought me up against all my insecurities. What if I couldn't do this?

Tim was one of the few people I trusted to see me and help me, although I was wary of his big personality that was laden with sarcasm and dark humor. I still trusted him more than anyone in my life. We found a respect for each other that kept our friendship strong through many challenges.

LOSING TIM

During the summer of 1995, I saw less of Tim. I was focused on my acting career while he was busy traveling around the country, healing people. In October, he stopped by to do some work at my place. He seemed troubled by something, and he wanted to spend some personal time with me. I was busy and only had limited time.

We finally connected on his last morning at my place. When I had to leave, he followed me to my car in the garage and kept talking to me as I pulled away. The last thing he said to me was, "I love ya, brother." He touched my arm. I said, "Love ya too," and drove away. I remember feeling funny, like he was really saying good-bye. He was.

Tim left Los Angeles and flew to Aspen, Colorado. He picked up a car he had purchased from a friend and headed back home to Sedona. Apparently, he fell asleep at the wheel and met a semi-truck, head-on, in Blanding, Utah. He died instantly.

I remember he said to me, "David, I am being called to fight a galactic battle against the Dark Forces. My karma is immediate. Everything I think and do is coming back to me immediately." I nodded yes, like I understood. Had he been talking about his impending death? I think back on this many times and realize it taught me a great lesson about really listening to a loved one and hearing what they have to say. You just never know what life may bring.

Tim was like a brother to me, and a father, and most of all, a good friend. Losing him was so hard for me, and it was difficult on his three children, who were of high school and college ages. I was close with the youngest, Danny. Every so often, Tim comes in loud and clear and asks me to check on Danny, so I make an effort to call or e-mail Danny, or find out how he is doing from friends.

What does this all mean? I still do not know. I just know that my life changed drastically when Ezekiel started waking me up, and after that time, I asked God to send me answers. I discovered so much about myself during the three or so years with Tim; it was an exciting and expansive time. Since he died, what he told me has made so much more sense. I had reservations about his statements that I was a healer and how I should write a book. Sometimes, I still have doubts about some of the other things he said. Yet, I do the writing.

Tim introduced me to Sedona, where he lived when not on the road. I love that place because of the strong energy vortexes. A vortex is an energy center for an area on the earth, much like a chakra on a person. I find that vortexes assist us in clearing blocked energy, and help us to balance. Sedona is an energy mecca, attracting people from all over the world. It has a reputation for being a New Age capital, and in a lot of ways, that is true. I tell people, "If you have a camera, it is worth the cost of getting there just to take pictures." It is an imposing landscape of gorgeous, red rock formations. Depending on the time of day, the sunlight creates stunning images with red sandstone sculptures created by the forces of nature. Within this visual beauty lies some of the most powerful energy confluences on the planet. I start vibrating as I drive into Sedona and experience amazing healing while I am there.

Now, I am at peace with being a healer. It has been quite a journey, and took several years before I gave in to the calling. I usually tell people that the earth is a "free will" zone, meaning we have the right to choose what we do in our lives. Yet in the last ten years, sometimes it feels as though I have no choice but to do the healing work. And I must admit, the work is the one thing that flows easily in my life. When I tell people from other places what I do, they say, "Healer? What's that?" Of course in Los Angeles, healers are more commonplace. I am comfortable calling myself a healer now in any situation. I guess I have arrived.

On March 17, 2000, I got married. My wife, Morgan, and I united after knowing each other only six short months. I learned so much about myself, and the choices that I made, in the three years we were together. Although I am pro-relationship and pro-marriage, this one ended at the three-year mark. Nonetheless, I am a truly a lucky man because I have an angel of a daughter, Ruby, and a salvageable friendship with my ex-wife.

That is my history.

HISTORY EXERCISE

Create a list of pivotal moments, decisions, and relationships in your life. Write down ten to twenty of them. After you compile the list, notice the road map that got you where you are today. Does it make sense? Does it seem like one accident or mistake after another? Or, does it flow in a way that uplifts you and brings understanding to your life?

In the chapters that follow, we will look at ways to break down your life and understand your approach to it. If you are not happy with your life or have a feeling you can do better, keep reading. We will unblock some areas, so that you can move forward. Many people tell me they have dealt with their past traumatic events. I often find that they do the psychological work, yet do not clear the energy out of their subconscious, their bodies, or their energy fields. We will look at ways to do that now.

Here is my list of pivotal moments, decisions, and relationships:

AGE 1 - 18
Loss of Jeffrey: sadness/grief
Catholic upbringing: restrictive and controlling
Farm life: hard work
Relationship with Dad: intense and volatile
Relationship with Granddad: easy and loving
Basketball: self-expression
Small school: small town mentality
Rebellious: when not seen or understood
Dad pulling shotgun on me: the "voice" arrived
Leaving home for college: the natural thing to do

AGE 19 - 46
Getting my MBA degree from University of Kentucky: staying in school
Leaving Kentucky: leaving the farm for good
Visiting California: I liked the West Coast
Taking a job in Florida: I liked the East Coast
Acting: learning about my emotions, self-discovery
Moving to Los Angeles: developing faith to trust that the universe will support me
Meeting Tim Heath: mentor for the healing work
Learning about Ezekiel: big shift in Spiritual awareness
Going to Sedona, Arizona with Tim: an energy mecca
Becoming a healer: finally
Getting married: finally
Buying a house: better than renting
Having our baby, Ruby: pure joy!
Getting a divorce: a big lesson about change and letting go

CHAPTER TWO

YOUR PERSONAL JOURNEY

This section, along with the Pyramid of Life section that follows, deals with the past, present, and future situations in your life. The approaches presented in these two sections explore psychology and psychotherapy, which is sometimes necessary to do before you can clear the channels to set your life in motion.

Life is full of opportunities to grow, to change expectations, and to change reality. How many of us truly seize these opportunities? What will happen if you deal with things to completion as they come up, right when you notice them, as they happen?

The true nature of Spirituality is clarity, presence, openness, and knowing yourself well enough to deal with issues, people, and experiences as they happen. Where are you in your life? Let us start by taking a look at your past.

THE PAST = PAIN

When you complete the exercise in the My History section, you will have the information necessary to complete this next exercise. If you have not completed this exercise, create lists of the following:

- Pivotal moments/decisions/relationships in your life

- Family dynamics/childhood experiences

- Romantic relationships —it's worth checking these again!

Refer to the previous sections for additional information to compile your lists. Be brave and honest in creating the lists.

THE PAST EXERCISE

Write down issues in these areas that need to be cleared up or resolved. Deal specifically with any unfinished pain from the past. When you think of an experience or a person and feel pain, discomfort, or resistance, recognize it as an area that needs to be cleared up. When you feel hesitancy, know there will be fruit to harvest with this clearing.

For instance, I had many childhood and adult issues with my father. As I studied these issues, I saw the similarities in my father and myself, and in much of the past. I recognized these similarities as my relationship got easier with him, and now there is acceptance. It took most of my forty-six years to do this. Recently, I have started to receive more letters and phone calls from my father. The shift has been ever so subtle, yet noticeable. Many times in the past, I grew frustrated when I initiated healing and communication and it was not acknowledged. I have learned that patience is a virtue.

Another example would be with cancer patients. I find they have definite unfinished business with their past, specifically, unresolved anger that may be steeped in denial. How can healing be facilitated soon enough to save their lives? Is death part of their destiny at this time? These are scientifically unanswerable questions, yet I believe they can be addressed Spiritually; not always with someone being healed in a physical sense, yet perhaps in a Spiritual one. Whichever the case, something in the past must be dealt with.

This came up with a mother in her thirties. A bright woman with two young children, and with a strong Spiritual side, she was in the latter stages of cancer treatment when she came to me. I knew we had to get to the core of her pain, and the "voice" said, "father." I asked her about the unresolved anger related to her father. Shaken, she said, "Do we have to get into that?" and I answered yes.

The woman was estranged from her dad and did not expect him to be available to her. I asked her to contact him and open the lines of communication, to ask him to come to her to assist in the healing. She did contact him, although she could not bring herself to ask for help.

Eventually, as she lay dying, her father made it to her bedside. My hope to intervene with the cancer was dashed. It is so important to deal with things as they happen, as soon as you become conscious of them, to avoid allowing issues to solidify into terminal illness (unless, of course, it is the soul's destiny).

Take action. Make phone calls, write letters and send e-mails. Confront people and situations face-to-face. Do it with love, and be honest with yourself and others. Explain what you are doing. If you need support, ask a partner or a close friend who wants to do the work with you. Do not wait for a day that feels better. Get the work done now.

THE FUTURE = FEAR

While past work deals with pain, the future is about fear. Fear is a very creative energy, and to deal with your fears, you must out-create this negative energy. To outsmart fear, make positive decisions and choices. The results can be remarkable.

+ Where are your greatest fears?

+ What, specifically, are you afraid of?

+ Where do you need more intention in your life?

- Intention is something that you plan to do, the state of having a purpose in mind. Purpose allows you to out-create the inactivity generated by fear. It provides you with a plan and resulting actions

THE FUTURE EXERCISE

Describe in writing all of your fears and their effects on your life. Let go. Write about everything that scares you. Let yourself as a little child appear with his or her scariest thoughts.

A wealthy client of mine was suffering from increasing anxiety about his money. Even though most of his investments were in real estate, the stock market plummet put him in a state of panic. After writing about all of his fears we found that he was most afraid of simply losing his money. Upon further exploration we discovered that his deep-seated fear of the future came from the fact that he had inherited his money, he didn't earn it. He had managed the money well and increased his wealth. Yet, he did not trust his ability to manifest money, and his family had continually reinforced the idea of "don't lose it." In effect, he had inherited both money and fear. Once we clarified this, he was better able to validate what he had accomplished with his inheritance. From there, he was able to have more intention about what he wanted to do with his fortune, and he realized that losing his money was not a reality at all.

Move with intent. Take the action necessary to face your fears. Surprise yourself, or better, shock yourself. Doing something about the fear always beats dwelling on the fear.

Draft a plan to grow beyond your fears and banish them. This may mean making budgets, making forecasts, and setting realistic goals. Businesses survive by using budgets, forecasts, and goals, but individuals or couples are often overwhelmed by the idea of these tools. Once they confront their fear around creating a budget and do it, the fear goes away. And, much of the fear around money goes away too. As they create the framework with a budget they get reality on their forecasted income and expenses. When reality moves them out of the unknown, where fear flourishes, they can set realistic goals about their lifestyle and their relationship with money.

> *A young artistic couple came to me complaining about breakdowns within their relationship. Most of the problems centered on an uncertainty with money. They lived hand-to-mouth and their income was unreliable. We were able to create a budget based on their known expenses, so they knew how much money they needed each month. Once we established those realities with their expenses, they started having fun with their earning potential and after a few months began putting money in the bank. It was fascinating how their relationship got better once their views and responsibilities about money got clear.*

If needed, make a collage or three-dimensional treasure map of your dreams. See the Collages section for additional information. The collage helps bring the dream into focus and lets the universe know what you want. A collage gives shape, form, and reality to an intention or dream. It clarifies the picture for a person about what they are creating in the future, as opposed to thinking about something, and being stifled by not being able to see how to achieve it. The collage can move an individual out of the Future = Fear mold and into the present.

> *A client who owned a successful plumbing business expressed a desire to grow large like some of the nationally known companies. He had opportunities to expand, yet was afraid to do so. I asked him to do a collage and show me his vision in as much detail as possible. Once he set aside the time to do this (plumbers are always on call), he started to get excited about his future. In doing the collage, he discovered his fears were*

*around growth, management, and personal time. These
issues needed planning and structuring with intention within his vision. His collage revealed managers, staff, offices, uni-
forms, vans, and plumbers. It also displayed vacation time
with family, and personal time for himself. Afterwards, he
said he never thought he had to be this specific. By doing so,
he was no longer afraid to let the company grow.*

Commit to what you can actually do and deliver. Remain in
the present, and be aware that you are dealing with an expected
future. The expected future is one tainted with fear, which is
often an illusion. Clarifying what we want in the future, based
on what is real right now, will out-create that fear.

Most people do not have confidence or faith around their
future, because they do not know how to validate their success-
es. Looking outside of yourself for validation creates uncertain-
ty about your future. Learn to validate yourself by focusing on
what is real to you right now.

The present moment is what is real.

THE PRESENT = PEACE

Here we are in present time, in the Spiritual realm of life. Be
aware of how much less energy it takes to be present—this is one
of the main goals of our work in this book. It is important that
you acknowledge how it feels to be present. Notice the difference between being in the present, and how you feel when you
work with the past and the future. Feel your power to choose
experiences. See how peaceful life can be.

Julia Cameron's book, *The Artist's Way*, has encouraged
many people to journal stream of consciousness pages each
morning as a form of healing and artistic expression. I have
referred many clients to this book over the years, and have seen
wonderful results. Stream of consciousness writing connects
you to your truth and can be powerful and freeing.

A few years ago, I was in a writing group where we met once
a week to work on our skills and commitment to writing. The
minimum requirement was to do morning pages each day. We

THE PRESENT EXERCISE

Write from a stream of consciousness about the subjects below. Just let your thoughts flow without judgment.

Gratitude: I have gratitude for my daughter, life, health, etc.

Love: I love my family, friends, God, nature, money, etc.

Joy: I have joy about this book, my life, friends, community, etc.

Stay in the present as you do this. Writing is a joyful relief when we are truly in the moment. Let the energy of each thought pass through you as you evoke Gratitude, Love, and Joy. Allow the process to be as effortless as light channeling through you, like the sun's rays striking morning dew. Do you spend enough time in the present being grateful, being in love, and being joyful?

worked as a group for six months, and so much creative work was completed that I have often wondered why we allowed the group to fold. A busy life is not a good reason to stop creating in this way. During this time, I witnessed people in the group open up and blossom Spiritually as well as creatively. It may be time to start another writing group!

SUMMARY: THE CALLING

I do not remember consciously calling for God to wake me up. Although a calling seemed to be an undercurrent of who I was, I had no idea of my calling. I know right and wrong, I know who I am, I know God, and know my heart; yet, I never knew I had a purpose until God chose me.

Do you know where you are in your life right now? Does it make sense to you? How do you feel about your journey? Are you on the path? To get somewhere in life, you need to understand where you came from.

Although we are all on separate paths to Healing and Spirituality, I believe that most of us will one day feel a calling to awaken our soul. Is it time for you to awaken?

Put out the call for your calling!

- Ask God to come in and bless it.

- Ask Archangel Michael to protect it.

- Ask your heart to keep it pure.

- Ask the fairies to give it magic.

- Ask the earth to give it roots.

- Ask your family, friends, and loved ones for support.

- Ask yourself for courage to act on it now.

- Have faith.

- Now go and travel in the Light!

Were there signs along my path of my calling as a healer? In the next section, I will talk about some of the signs and strange occurrences I experienced once I became aware enough to notice and make the connections.

STRANGE OCCURRENCES

Of the many unusual experiences I have had, none are about alien abductions. However, I believe that I have seen a few aliens passing themselves off as humans. Fortunately, they did not seem to be interested in me.

STARLIGHT

Stars and lights in the sky have become a part of my life. In 1997, I moved from Los Angeles to New Mexico. On my last night in Los Angeles, I woke up at 3:00 a.m. and went outside to check my truck and trailer. Due east up in the sky towards New Mexico, I saw a twinkling star. As I watched, the star tripled in size and began moving toward me, toward Los Angeles. I watched it for a while, and then it vanished. This and other strange occurrences have happened at pivotal moments in my life when I was unsettled, unsure, or making changes in my life.

Previously in 1995, while camping at Devil's Tower in South Dakota, I woke up again at 3:00 a.m. As I gazed at the stars and thought about my life and about a relationship, I saw a twin-kling star directly overhead. I watched it fall, blazing due south. I was awed, and wanted to share this with someone! My companions, Jody and her daughter Clara, were sound asleep.

I looked up again to see the same star, twinkling again. It twinkled like crazy and then it fell due north. What was that? I was thinking about my life when the star fell. Was the star saying I would be happy?

After this, I began to awaken every morning at 3:00 a.m. I knew something was up, and I asked God, "What am I supposed to receive?" The response was, "Write," so I kept a pad and a pen by the bed. The more I wrote, the easier and faster I got back to sleep. Then the message changed to, "Go outside and look up at the sky." So wherever I was, I got up and looked at the sky. Virtually every time, I saw a falling star within a few seconds. I had no idea what that meant, and I still do not. This went on for a couple of months and still occurs occasionally.

One night in New Mexico when I was about to move back to Los Angeles, a star followed my movements and seemed to twinkle or blink every time I noticed it or focused on it. Two friends from New Mexico, John and Donald, noticed it, too. I dismissed the experience, thinking it was just another coincidence. Nonetheless, I have noticed my connection with stars since my healing work began. A healer friend of mine said, "You are a messenger. They are trying to communicate with you." I said, "Who are they?" He just looked at me as if I should already know.

Sometimes I feel like Richard Dreyfus in the movie, *Close Encounters of the Third Kind*. I know I am being led somewhere and there seems to be a sort of destiny involved, though there are no definite answers that I can pass on about the stars yet. Nevertheless, I do not resist so much now. I try to embrace whatever I see and feel, even though some of it is a little unusual.

As I think back at pivotal moments in my life, there was always a distinct sense of awareness, such as the memory of the death of my baby brother, Jeffrey, or the "voice" revealing itself when my dad pulled his shotgun on me. I believe that everyone has a certain awareness and has experiences such as mine, but most people ignore them. You may have been touched by Spirit and may not remember or have noticed.

FLIGHT OF THE HAWK

I also have repeated occurrences and connections with red-tailed hawks. They fly around me every day, circling me wherever I am and whenever I am doing healing work, arriving at a supreme moment of truth with a client. At these moments, a hawk will appear, screaming overhead. Spirit shoots through me every time.

In January of 2003, I was working in Manhattan out of a fifth-floor apartment. I was with a lady and we were at a key moment in her session. Her heart opened, Spirit moved, I got goose bumps and I noticed a hawk circling the building, fifteen feet from the window. I could hear it screeching along with the sounds of the city. I had the woman sit up and look at the hawk. I am sure it was more meaningful to me than her.

But after years of this happening, I pay attention when Spirit moves and the hawks show up. It is always a validation to me that I am paying attention to the signs from above. For me, this is always about being firmly rooted in the moment.

My adventures with hawks began to happen in the early days with Tim, my mentor. He had lots of bird feathers and I was drawn to his hawk feathers. Also, when I was at home in Kentucky, I saw a huge red-tailed hawk, the biggest hawk I had ever seen, on a fence post on my dad's farm. I stopped the truck and looked at it. The bird looked at me. I said, "I would love to have some feathers, but I will not kill you for them." He flew away.

A week later, back in California while walking with my two friends Madeline and Tom down a country road in Ojai, I heard a sound and looked up. A feather floated towards me, just like in the movie *Forrest Gump*. I caught it. My friends looked at me, and then about twenty feet in front of us, a hawk fell to the ground. His eyes were smoking! I looked up at a telephone pole and realized that the bird had been electrocuted. I didn't think that was ever supposed to happen. The feather I caught had blown out of his wing from the jolt of electricity.

My friends stared at me. When I told them about the hawk in Kentucky, they said the hawk was my medicine, and they asked for a tail feather. I told them to pull out a feather, which was not easy. I had to grip the feathers hard and twist—I was the only one who could harvest the feathers.

When we got back to the house, Tim was there. He said, "Let's get the hawk. It is your medicine. You need to take it with you." He said we could give it to a Native American friend of ours for safekeeping. I wanted to bury the bird, and eventually, I did. It is illegal to have hawk feathers unless you are Native American.

Since these episodes, hawks have followed me, just like the owls that follow Harry in the *Harry Potter* movies. In the book *Medicine Cards* by Sams and Carson, the hawk is referred to as the messenger. The phrase, "You're a messenger," started to make sense to me. I watch hawks and I relate to them. I whistle their cry and they seem to be curious, circling me.

If I whistled to the twinkling stars and they came down, would I like that? More than just a coincidence, their twinkling and their movements seem to be an attempt to communicate with me. Someday, I hope to find out what that is all about.

DOLPHIN ENCOUNTERS

Dolphins got my attention in 1986, just before my healing adventure out West was about to start. I went to Key Largo, Florida, to swim with dolphins at a "Swim with Wild Dolphins" facility. I was told the dolphins were wild, and free to return to the ocean at any time. They are tempted with all the fish they can eat, and swimming with humans is supposed to be a delight for them. The dolphins were around 500 or 600 pounds, and primarily interested in the fish.

We listened to a thirty-minute talk on do's and don'ts, including, "Don't touch the dolphins unless they touch you," and a warning that male dolphins can be very aggressive towards women. They can grab a wrist with their mouth and teeth and attempt to mate. Good thing I'm a guy!

After the lecture, we entered the water to swim free with the dolphins. Occasionally a dolphin is known to interact with a swimmer, and we were told to be ready if this happened. While trying to figure out my snorkeling equipment, the next thing I knew, I had a dolphin on either side of me, within six inches of my face. They rolled past, eyeball-to-eyeball with me, then stopped and looked at me. They continued to stare at me for several minutes, and I was mesmerized—afraid I would drown— but definitely mesmerized. The creatures made noises, sending sonar beeps through my brain for a minute or two. I heard people yelling and I lifted my head out of the water. The instructors were yelling, "They've accepted you, reach out and touch them." Too late, I splashed back down into the water; they had moved away.

I will never forget my moments with the dolphins, an ancient feeling, as those eyeballs rolled back in their heads to look at me. They sent sonar through my brain as if downloading something into me. Perhaps it was healer data or the activation of memories and instincts to be used as a healer. Shortly after this experience, my life as a healer began. I know something happened in that exchange between my brain and the two dolphins. No one helps me interpret this, although the "voice" humorously hints that something did happen.

Another time, I was on a beach in Malibu under a full moon, after midnight, telling my friend Jody and my sister Julie about my experience swimming with the dolphins. Just then, a pod of dolphins showed up forty or fifty feet offshore. They chirped and called me out into the water. Not a great swimmer, I was too scared to enter the dark, rough water. I knew they had something to tell to me, and I regret not connecting with them that night. I know now that I would have been protected; I did not know it then.

STRANGE OCCURRENCES EXERCISE

Get out your notebook.

What are the strangest occurrences that have happened to you? Think about what was happening in your life at those times. Was Spirit leading you to where you actually ended up, or is it still trying to lead you elsewhere? Are you starting to suspect that there is another destiny for you this lifetime? If you could get out of the way with your will, your intellect, and your fears, you might just be led to it. Open yourself up to these questions. See what reveals itself and write it down.

SPIRITUAL TEACHERS

In 1987, I quit the corporate world, moved to Los Angeles, and committed myself to acting, which proved to be an excellent Spiritual teacher: a playground for self-discovery and growth. At first, painfully shy about expressing myself emotionally and artistically, I allowed acting to seize me by the balls and take me for a ride.

The work was exciting, Spiritually difficult, and invaluable to my development. This was not about getting famous, it was about getting to know myself and being able to exercise my feelings freely. All of my acting teachers were Spiritual teachers, who helped actors find their truth. I learned to tap in and use myself as an instrument. Although I have let acting go for now, I will do it again if the time is right.

My next biggest teacher was my old friend and Spiritual teacher Tim Heath, who called himself a "mystic" healer. And, although he had tremendous insights and gifts as a healer, he was not a saint. He had a well-developed human side with a myriad of issues and flaws available for scrutiny.

Tim was a triple Scorpio and could lay a person open like a laser. He did not always put them back together smoothly. With incredible intuitive senses he would take people to the depths of their pain and blockages, often resulting in the people wondering what hit them. Even though their experiences with him were phenomenal, they sometimes would end up having hard times making sense of it. And Tim had little patience for their fear and doubt as it started to creep back in. I think he got bored holding their hands through the completion of the healing process.

I learned so much from the way he worked and from the way he lived, which was always for the moment and with little concern for future responsibilities, especially finances. Tim came with psychic gifts and great psychic receptivity; nonetheless, he had a fair amount of psychic static and distortion in the areas of finance and sex. He was often lazy with his ethics in those two areas.

Consequently, I saw Tim's clients, friends, and family become disenchanted with him, and they set out to take him down with gossip and psychic attacks, criticism and slander. He had an amazing ability to forgive and forget, much easier than I would. He would smile at them, feed them, forgive them, and love them. I watched this over and over.

I saw the dichotomy, yet I know what this man's love did for me. He taught me how to love, forgive, play, and be a man. So, regardless of the stories that exist about Tim the man, I love him both for the message he delivered and the messenger he was. Life has been different without him. And wherever you are Tim, I still feel your love and support. I am still here for you, brother.

SPIRITUAL GUIDES AND TEACHER EXERCISE

+ Who were your Spiritual guides and teachers?

+ Have you acknowledged them for their love and support?

+ Have you acknowledged them within yourself?

+ Were you aware of their human side?

+ Did that drive you away?

+ Were you able to receive their message?

SPIRITUAL REVIEW EXERCISE

+ Review your Spiritual Journey.

+ Review your Pivotal Moments/Decisions.

+ Try and connect the dots. See if you can allow your intuition to come through and reveal your heart's desire. Is there something you are being guided to do with your life?

+ Is there anything that you continue to deny in your journey?

+ Identify the points where you have felt the most at peace with yourself.

+ Are you still waiting for something to happen?

THE PYRAMID OF LIFE

I created this pyramid to illustrate where people spend most of their time, energy, and consciousness. From the bottom up, right? My goal with this work is to bring freedom to people so they can choose where (which level) they want to be in their life. Freedom comes from being able to choose. If your past or future is imprisoning you, your choices may be limited. The more you stimulate the process of awareness, the easier it will be. Clear yourself of unwanted, unconscious, parasitic energies. Where awareness goes, energy flows. Through the Personal Journey and the Pyramid of Life, I give you tools to bring awareness to yourself and be free.

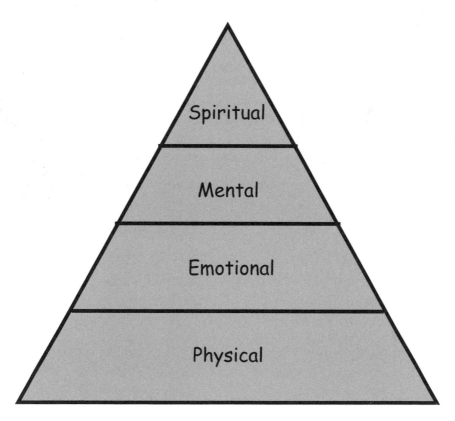

Figure 1. The Four Levels of the Pyramid of Life

The Pyramid of Life is broken into four levels, each constantly shifting and changing in focus and balance. As you climb the various levels, you may or may not have mastered the lower levels. You will find that when the lower levels are balanced, it is easier to remain balanced in the upper levels.

PHYSICAL LEVEL

The physical level is the starting point, relating to the survival of our bodies and physical energy. Many people spend so much of their time caring for this level that they have little left for the others.

Challenges on the Physical Level

+ Physical handicaps

+ Diseases, life-threatening and chronic conditions

+ Obsessions with the body, addiction to working out, plastic surgery, etc.

+ Anorexia, bulimia, obesity

+ Mundane issues of diet, exercise, sex

The Physical Level is your foundation. When it is dysfunctional, you will find it difficult to work on the other levels, especially the Spiritual Level. Some of my biggest challenges on the Physical Level have been ankle sprains from playing basketball. When I experienced severe pain, I primarily stayed on the Physical and Emotional Levels. This realization gave me more compassion for people in pain, especially when they are grumpy and negative. I understand how pain creates a reality that becomes a constant experience.

Even though I believe that physical pains, injuries, and ailments are manifestations of Spiritual imbalances, I still work with and address the Physical Level with my clients. One client, Johnny J, was a gifted musician. The only time he was not in physical (lower back) pain was when he was playing his music. He went to every healer in town and tried every detox program. He saw doctors and surgeons, with doctors wanting to rehabilitate and surgeons wanting to operate. He was bored with physical therapy and scared of surgery. I suggested we address all the levels of the Pyramid of Life, starting with the Physical Level. He was in lousy shape, though he used to have a trainer who was trying to strengthen his stomach muscles. So, he recommitted to training and started a spinning/exercise class to help with conditioning.

He and I dealt with a chip he carried on his shoulder about always getting screwed in life, which greatly affected his physical, emotional, mental, and Spiritual levels of existence. This chip kept him stuck in the past; he was stuck, and his energy was stuck in his back. Metaphorically, his energy was stuck BACK there somewhere. I really focused on this chip, because I knew it was blocking much of his creative and Spiritual flow. We had big breakthroughs, and he stayed with the exercise program. Suddenly, his back started to get better and his music started to happen. Emotionally, he expressed much more happiness even when he was not playing his music. With his pain greatly reduced, his mental clarity improved, and he started writing more songs. His music turned a corner and he found himself generating a positive, upbeat message with his tunes. I looked at his recovery as a Spiritual rehabilitation; he looked at his recovery as a physical one. To ascend the pyramid, we started at the bottom and worked our way up.

Ways to Strengthen the Physical Level

- Rest, get bodywork, eat healthy, work out, cleanse/detox, do yoga, play sports.

- As you get stronger in the physical level, you will be able to move up the pyramid and seek out more healing in the other levels.

- Balance with the other levels.

I try to keep my ankles in good shape. I work out regularly and do some exercise, such as basketball, spinning, weight training, mountain biking, or yoga, every day. Most of my ankle sprains occur when I am angry, so I do not play basketball when I am angry. In addition to exercise, I consistently eat live, healthy, organic foods, and take supplements to enhance my diet to get all the nutrition my body needs. I also do a cleanse twice a year in the spring and fall. A cleanse is a detox program enhanced by supplements and very clean live foods. It is generally not a fast; a fast is its own type of cleanse, and it is a very intense one.

Questions for the Physical Level

- Where are you with your Physical Level?

- Are you in touch and connected with your body?

- Do you place too little or too much emphasis on the body?

- Are you balanced?

- What will it take to get your physical body and energy straightened out? Are you poisoning yourself with addictive substances like drugs, alcohol, cigarettes, coffee, chocolate, sugar, and junk food?

If you feel balanced and at ease on the Physical Level, move on to the Emotional Level. If not, focus on this level more and see if you can get clear with it.

EMOTIONAL LEVEL

This second level on the pyramid is very powerful. Many people live their lives on an emotional roller coaster, and are stuck on the Emotional Level to the detriment of all other levels. The Mental and the Spiritual Levels do not provide enough adrenaline for them. Emotions can lock people into past or future events, and they miss the power of the moment. Intellect looks forward, emotions look back, and the body is in the present.

Maureen, a thirty-eight-year-old single woman, was an admitted emotional junky when she came to see me. She was looking for a quick fix to her relationship woes. She said most of her relationships ended at the three-month mark. At this point the sex dried up and the romance ended. Usually at this time the big emotional blowup would occur, driving the other person away for good.

Although Maureen said she was ready to end this cycle, I was not so sure. We talked about her emotions, and she explained that she was an emotional person, an artist, whose emotions often swung from high to low—an emotional addict remaining stuck in the previous experiences of her life. In therapy for years, she had been sedated by a wide variety of sleep medications, and antidepressant and antianxiety drugs. She had gone to a new therapist who turned her down, saying, "I can't help you. You have done it all and nothing worked. Go see this healer."

When she came to me, I told her that antidepressants were not the solution, and that our early work was crucial and we needed to go directly to the problem.

Maureen referred to her father as an alcoholic. I said to her, "Tell me something new." She said, "I am a sugar addict, but I don't think I could be an emotional addict, do you?" Well rehearsed from her years of therapy, she used her emotions to remain a little girl, unable to take responsibility for being a woman. A smart girl/woman, she finally began to understand her behavior and her mind-set. Once we cleared this hurdle, it was easier to address the different levels of the pyramid with her. When she chose to take responsibility for her emotions, it was easy for her to deal with all levels of her life. I did not tell her to avoid having emotions; rather, I told her to be aware of how she used them.

Challenges on the Emotional Level
- Stuck in life by being too emotional; reactive to external stimuli; use of illusions to support being stuck

- Emotional shutdown, unable to feel anything

People stuck on this level are unable to confront their fears and communicate with others honestly and forthrightly. They may be very emotional, or they may withhold their emotions. Whichever the case, they do this to get their way. Babies have a right to live in this level, but adults do not.

The biggest challenge for me on the Emotional Level has been to create deep, intimate friendships wherein I can share my innermost feelings. I keep much to myself, and therefore work at being more emotional than I feel comfortable being. Emotional distance is a Capricorn trait and I know that it is beneficial to me to be more emotionally open.

Ways to Strengthen the Emotional Level
- Be active, move through your feelings so you are not stuck in them.

- To move through your feelings or get unstuck, stay focused with intention. Choose to move to another level to bring about this shift. Exercise/physical, think/mental, meditate/Spiritual. Do it with intention and freedom will come.

- Be aware of your acts or manipulations and resolve not to use them.

- When it is hard to express your emotions freely, then write in a journal about them.

Acting and healing work strengthen me on this level. Acting is a workout for my emotions, and when I do healing work, all of the emotional states of being are mirrored to me. For example, when I am feeling a particular emotion, a client often walks in the door needing to work through that same emotion. One day, I was feeling sad over not seeing my daughter as much since my divorce. Later that day, a client came in who had just lost his two-year-old son to an accident. It touched a deep sense of compassion inside of me and brought me to a place of gratitude for each moment I was able to spend with my daughter.

Healing work and acting help me stay active and move through my emotions. I also set intentions, which are plans to do something, about most of what I do in life. Setting intentions helps keep me focused and active on the Emotional Level.

Questions for the Emotional Level

- Are you stuck in your emotional life, e.g. angry all the time, anxious, impatient, or depressed?

- Can you consciously shift to other levels in the pyramid to get unstuck with your emotions?

- If you are stuck, are you willing to keep a journal and write about your emotional life?

- Would you be willing to talk about your emotions? Try talking to a friend or someone safe about your emotions.

The more awareness you bring to this area, the more choice you can exhibit over how it goes. As this happens, it releases you to be freer with your emotions and you will not be afraid of them taking over or exposing you in a detrimental way. Emotions can move through you as a flow of energy, which can be liberating and empowering.

MENTAL LEVEL

The Mental Level sets us apart as a species. This level does not come without its contradictions and duplicity for those committed to the Spiritual Level. The more developed a person is intellectually, the bigger the temptation to remain at this level. The Mental Level may prove to be more comfortable than the Emotional or Spiritual Levels for many people.

Challenges on the Mental Level
- ◆ Getting stuck in this level, to the detriment and demise of all other levels

- ◆ Being so mental that you have very little connection to the physical body; an example would be a "nerd" or a "computer geek"

- ◆ Cannot be emotional without fear of losing control—the development of the intellect is in place to protect a painfully shy sensitive side

- ◆ Being Spiritual may be good in theory only; there is no willingness to venture into this realm; skepticism is safer

My biggest challenge on this level is a combination of emotional and mental circumstances. For example, I may be afraid (Emotional) of something and get stuck in my head (Mental) as I try to figure it out or control it, such as writing this book. At first, I was unsure if it would be good enough, and that stopped me from writing. My brain froze in confusion. Eventually, just the physical act of continuing to write set my Mental Level free.

Ways to Strengthen the Mental Level
While balance is important on all levels, it is imperative on the Mental Level. While the mind can be like a vice, the Mental Level must be open, bright, and flexible. Open-mindedness is a term that reflects so much. It means a person is open to receive, to experience, and to give. This exemplifies love and allows Light to illuminate life.

Once Johnny J, the musician mentioned earlier, opened physically, it was easier for him to ascend the pyramid to open emotionally and mentally. As he wrote more songs, Spirit came in and touched his music. Mentally he opened to the message that was coming. It took him to some great Spiritual experiences with his life and career. Everything was connected. Some might say it was the songs that did it, others might say it was something else, but he believed it was the healing of his back. I believe it was the reclamation of his Spirit as we healed the way he looked back at his life, in which the Mental Level was very important.

To strengthen this level, I go to the Spiritual Level and set the Mental Level free. With faith and intention, I open and let in the Light, and my mind relaxes. When I have done my work, my mind is free to create and play. I also balance and pay attention to the Physical and Emotional Levels, because as I ascend the Pyramid, all the levels interact and link with each other.

Questions for the Mental Level

- ♦ Where are you with your Mental Level?

- ♦ Do you use this level to avoid certain feelings and realizations with the other levels? Are you rigid and judgmental?

- ♦ Do you have a lot of wrinkles around your forehead and eyebrow region? This could be a telltale sign of too much mental activity. Too much strain trying to figure everything out and a lack of trust of the flow of life.

Challenge yourself to get out of your head, let yourself feel, and confront your life. Once Johnny J, the musician, was stuck with his back pain, he realized he was stuck overall. He said he had "gone mental" and could not get himself out. He was not making music, for he was focused on back pain. This is similar to when a baseball player goes into a slump. He knows it is mental. He goes to the hitting coach who takes him back to the basics, and they work through the technique to get him hitting without thinking. Confidence comes from being able to demonstrate to yourself that you can handle any situation without being stopped by fear or thinking about failure.

SPIRITUAL LEVEL

The most sought-after mysteries are found on the Spiritual Level, the most elusive of all the levels. Most of us desire to be and feel Spiritual. The irony is that this level can exist on its own without help from the other levels. Nonetheless, to maintain this level with ease takes balance on all four of the levels.

When I talk about Spirit or my Spiritual connection, I mean my connection to God and the feeling I have in my heart about the God "out there" or "up there" that flows through me. If you do not like using the word "God," use Spirit, Light, Higher Power, or Nature. Use whatever name you like. For me, the source is the same, no matter what we call it or who we are.

Challenges on the Spiritual Level

+ Lack of awareness on how to reach the Spiritual Level

+ Skepticism about this level—"It's New Age crap, woo-woo, airy-fairy, Los Angeles/Sedona stuff."

+ Lack of desire to do the work to get there

My biggest challenge on the Spiritual Level is when I forget who I am and what I know. It feels like amnesia. Know the feeling? I talk about Spiritual awareness as "being." Being is consciousness taken one step at a time. At any step, if I feel I am unconscious, stuck, or lost, I fall out of the Spiritual realm. It is always my choice to become conscious of Spirit again and to remember what I know.

Ways to Strengthen the Spiritual Level

+ Balance and heal the lower levels

+ Connect, love, and develop faith about the journey

To strengthen my connection to the Spiritual Level, I maintain balance, openness, and healing on the other three levels. My connection to the Spiritual Level is strongest when I teach healing to a group, do the healing work, love, and experience gratitude and joy.

The group experience is magical. Like individuals, a group has a consciousness too. When people come together there is a common reason, known or unknown. All the group work I lead results from a communicated intention. That is our starting point. Once that has been relayed to the group members, it starts to work both on the conscious mind (known), and the unconscious mind (unknown). People feel the call of Spirit. They do not always know why they are called, and strong work will always create plenty of resistance to be worked through on physical, emotional, and mental levels. As that is accomplished, the Spiritual Level can be accessed with more ease as people trust themselves to show up at the top of the pyramid.

Questions for the Spiritual Level

- Where are you in connection with your Spiritual Level? Can you access it?

- What do you have left for this Level? Do the other three levels consume you?

- Do you feel the calling of your Spirit?

My connection to this level in my life has set me free, allowing me to heal and recharge, and providing me with answers to the questions of the other three levels. My Spiritual connection recharges my batteries.

Now that you have completed the first part of the book, continue with your personal work. It will help your life. The more you heal, the more you will be able to help others.

In the introduction, I said my intention was to show you how we are all healers. In the next chapter, I will share with you what I do as a healer. You will receive helpful insights and ideas, whether or not you think of yourself as a healer. So, read on and enjoy this information that has brought me great joy over the years.

PYRAMID OF LIFE SUMMARY EXERCISE

- Can you use the Pyramid of Life to evaluate your life?

- How honest can you be with yourself?

- Are you really doing your life... living it to the fullest?

- Is skepticism easier than doing the work?

- What price can you put on Spiritual freedom?

- If you are reading this book, it means you truly are looking for answers to your condition. Can you trust yourself to confront your true value to yourself, your family, and the world?

- Are you ready to work?

If so, keep reading so you can create the life you want. I promise you there are no accidents to the way your life is unraveling. Go with the flow, and trust it. If you can apply this section and use it as a tool to set yourself free, we all will benefit from that. As Martin Luther King, Jr. proclaimed, "Free at last!"

CHAPTER THREE

COMPONENTS OF THE WORK

A s time passes each day, I understand my reluctance to be a healer a little bit more. In the beginning, I was terrified by the responsibility of being a healer, of being responsible for people looking to me for help. What if I did not measure up? What if nothing happened and they were unhappy with me? It just seemed like too much. Then one summer day in 1996 a light went on. I was in the mountains of New Mexico having a nice breathing meditation alone under a huge ponderosa pine tree. I relaxed and went very deep. I thought I was asleep. Somewhere in the process I felt a tremendous opening, connecting me to nature—I could see it all. There were cobwebs of energy streaming out from me to the trees, grass, and sky. My third eye was very hot, energy was pouring into it and back out of my body. The "voice" said, "The work is not about you. You are a conduit, acting as a witness to God's work." I finally got it. What a relief! If I just hold the space, God does the work. Once I believed this, I began to understand what faith meant to me—faith that a higher power is available to help lead people to the Light.

My healing work is an active demonstration of faith. This understanding takes away my stress and worry about doing the work. All I have to do is show up. I do not need business cards or advertising. I do not need to take notes. It's easy.

Of course, the "voice" said, "We tried to tell you this all along, and you would not listen." In fact, that is how I decided on the title for this book—it describes my journey. Working through my reluctance, I grew to be less reluctant and more accepting of my job here on earth as a healer: as a healer who writes; as a writer who can act; as an actor who farms; as a farmer who is a father. When I think about all the things I do, I see less need for reluctance in my life. Now, I give in and do what I do best.

ENERGY

What is energy? A hip word for the New Millennium, we hear about energy all the time. Everyone is trying to find his or her energy. They look to yoga, meditation, exercise, music, art, sex, relationships, nature, dreams, their bodies, and their minds. So what is it?

I describe energy as electrical, vibrating sensations that flow through the body. These can vary from soft, ticklish sensations to strong pulsating vibrations that feel electrical. Energy is a combination of vitality, life force, personality, attitude, and intention. I work with a client's energy to balance it and raise the vibration. When I talk about raising the energy, I am referring to accelerating it and raising it up the chakra system, or higher in the body. For instance, moving the energy out of the pelvis or belly and up to the heart. If a person's energy is low, I tell them to get off their butt and do something. Be active. Be alive.

You need to find your energy, get familiar with it, and work with it to heal. I am an advocate of whatever helps bring people home to their energy. It may not be yoga or meditation that helps you find your energy; do whatever works for you to connect to it.

When I am feeling low-energy, I get instant results when I exercise. Recently, I was in a lethargic period. It was January: the holidays were over, I had another birthday, and I was indulging in sugar. It was also raining, so I had not been playing basketball—I had been sitting on my butt, and my energy was low. (Maybe you can relate.) I finally started exercising with a few hikes, a basketball game, and riding my mountain bike. When I was active again, my energy returned, and my confidence picked up as I felt clearer and stronger. Being active and exercising helps keep my energy level up.

> *Rick, a young real estate agent, came to see me and he looked horrible. I asked him what was going on. He said he had been in the feeding frenzy of the real estate market, was making lots of money, and thought he was doing great. I hated to burst his bubble, but I said, "You look like you're strung out on something." He admitted that he was run-down and needed rest. He took a few days off and went surfing. When he came back he realized how important surfing and time to himself was to his energy and well-being. The adrenaline rush from making a lot of money was seductive, and it was draining him of his own life force. Taking a break let him put things into perspective and probably saved him some problems down the road.*

I feel the most energy when my heart is open. I am in the moment, focused on something larger than I am, such as nature, art, creativity, children, and God. I love to feel energy. It makes me feel alive. Energy connects me to Spirit. I feel the most energy when I feel the most Spirit. They are all connected—Energy, Spirit, Heart, Love, Openness, Creativity, Imagination, Healing, and God.

Is it possible to maintain this connection all of the time? The meditation of life, and ultimately the art of life, is to maintain this connection in our everyday life. This is especially true in the big city, on our jobs, and in the most mundane moments of our lives. Choosing to stay connected to my energy in everything I do is a reality for me. Anything involving the illusions of life is not the real world to me.

People may describe their "real world" as the things they have to do or deal with in their life, such as jobs, mortgage payments, in-laws, traffic, and taxes. I see these things as the illusions they create to define their lives, rather than the "real world." It is easier to get sucked into illusions in big cities where there is more distraction, more static electricity, more pollution, more expense, more of everything. Cities have a distinct energy and rhythm all their own and it is easy to get sucked into that energy.

Once you are connected to your energy and are comfortable with feeling it, the fun begins. From there, you can learn how to work with energy, how to use it to heal, to intuit and interpret life. Energy is amazing that way—it is the pipeline to your sixth sense, your intuitive powers.

HEALING

Here are some questions that may occur to you:

+ What is healing?

+ Is it a momentary change or permanent?

+ Who determines if I am a healer? Me? My clients?

+ How do healings occur?

+ Is there a system or structure to the healing work?

+ Can I be trained to be a healer?

+ Can my instincts and intuition be developed?

If you still do not believe you can be a healer, keep reading. If you think you already have enough trouble taking care of yourself, let alone others, you may need this book more than those who believe they are healers. Remember, we are all healers in some way. You may not use all the healing techniques described in the book; you may find that some are useful in healing yourself, while some are more appropriate for healing others. Start with yourself. Heal yourself. Free yourself from fears and illusions about life. Give yourself permission to participate in life again or maybe for the first time.

What does the word "healer" mean to you? What does it mean to me? Does it mean someone who jumpstarts a person's natural process of healing? Or is it literally "someone who heals"?

I see myself as someone who assists people in healing. I find it difficult to heal people when they attempt to give me all the power. I want them to rediscover and awaken the power to heal themselves, not give it to me. The responsibility for healing and the choice to heal lies within each person. I can assist, stimulate, spark, reveal, and uncover elements that help in the healing process, but I am neither a magician nor Jesus, for that matter. As far as I know, I cannot turn water into wine.

I believe many people can be trained to do healing work, and this has been successfully demonstrated in the Healer Training courses, which are described in Appendix 1. Most importantly, I see tremendous personal growth in those who learn to do this work. And this is what I offer to you—great personal advancement and freedom as you focus on helping others. This is a simple concept: the floodgates of creativity open when you take the focus off yourself.

As a healer, I am guided by my intuition, which I believe is given to me from a higher realm such as God, Spirit, angels, or Nature. Sometimes I say my intuition guides me, via such elements as goose bumps, a feeling, a picture, or the "voice." The "voice" is the voice of intuitive guidance through the Clairaudience. I specify the "voice" because I have learned to pay special attention to its direction. I mention this now because I will make several references to it throughout the book.

During my years of healing work, some things happened that scared me about the word "power." One of the very first one-on-one sessions caused me concern. A friend called me and asked me to see Susan, who was apparently in great need. Reluctantly (of course), I agreed. Susan was a young, thin, pale, blonde woman in a very stressful and controlling relationship. She had been in therapy but still felt stuck. After talking with her and gathering information, I found out that she was adopted. My intuition told me this played a role in her current relationship and in the condition of her body. She was turned inward, obviously holding on to fear and pain. I immediately felt her anxiousness.

After hearing her story, I started to work with her energy, and located a major block in her pelvis above her ovaries. When I touched her stomach and hip bones, she jumped and sighed. She held a lot of tension here, and my intuition said this area was a host for drama and emotional volatility. She said her boyfriend was forcing her to have sex and that he was very jealous. Working with her energy and asking questions, I found a belief held in her body that "love had to be controlled, it could not be trusted." She admitted she never trusted men, especially her boyfriend. Sex was something she participated in yet rarely enjoyed.

As we focused on this, Susan's body did a purge, an emotional vomit. She cried, screamed, sobbed, and then nearly fell asleep. Spirit moved. Then, she remembered sitting on her adoptive father's lap when she was six. He told her, "No man will ever love you like I do." There appeared to be sexual connotations to the statement: when she talked about this memory, there was a sexual vibe in the air that was sticky and laden with guilt. The "voice" told me this was it.

Was she more susceptible to being controlled by this statement because she was adopted? Some part of her still believed what her adoptive father told her. She laid there in front of me, a little girl who felt unworthy of love, looking for her adoptive father's love. She was trapped on that Emotional Level, and I was not sure if I could get her beyond it. I almost yelled, "Stop that, snap out of it!" Then, I realized she was no longer with me. She was non-responsive, back there in the energy of that experience. She began to look even frailer. I realized that I needed to bring her back to the present from where she was, in the power of that place, memory, feeling, and energy. She was in the seductive web of sexual abuse.

Then, something shifted. My awareness, my feelings, and my focus were able to get energy moving through this blockage, which was created by a fear-based thought that love was controllable. I was able to get the energy to shift by clearly seeing/sensing it. This is one of my gifts as a healer. As this blocked energy started moving, I realized it was important for Susan to be guided through this process to do the actual work of uncovering the unconscious blocks in her body. And the amazing thing was, as her energy moved, she awoke from her stupor and she was suddenly right with me. The room was full of Spirit. We both got goose bumps and she started to cry.

The healing that occurred with Susan resulted in her uncovering the control of the sexual abuse energy. This energy was no longer able to hide, or to feed off of her energy like a parasite. Once this energy was uncovered it lost most of its power and ability to control her.

Susan said she had never trusted her adoptive father because he wanted her to do things that she knew were wrong. He always wanted her to sit on his lap and he would touch her inappropriately. As she talked about this, her Spirit began to return and she started to glow. I saw a golden light shimmering around her; she looked like an angel.

Susan healed a deep unconscious belief that love was about control and being controlled. She believed she had to do these things to receive love. I asked her where her adoptive mom was during all this, and she said she could not remember. Her adoptive father was older and her mom was afraid of him. Her mother had a history of being abused too. I looked at the power of this energy within Susan and her lineage. This unconscious belief was deep in her body, and had possibly been stored for many lifetimes in the soul of her being. Perhaps it took this lifetime of being adopted by a questionable father to bring her karmic pattern to the surface and to experience a dramatic shift. I was the witness. When she left, I had a profound feeling of accomplishment.

A couple of days later, Susan called and left me a message. She was very excited and told me what she had not been able to say during our session. A few days before she saw me, she had a medical procedure for some pelvic or ovarian cysts. On her checkup visit after our work, the doctors found no scarring from the procedure. They said it was a miracle that she healed that way. She believed this was a result of our work.

When I heard this message, it scared me. I thought, "Do I want this power?" I avoided seeing clients again for months. However, people persisted and they kept coming, learning about the work through word-of-mouth.

At that time, I was busy setting up healing groups and retreats for Tim, doing construction work, and acting in television and low-budget movies. A couple of the movies were sexy R-rated movies for cable TV, films that pushed my Catholic upbringing to its limit and taught me a lot about my views of sex and sexuality. Although I was able to keep busy and forget about being a healer for a while, it kept closing in. People that I met in all walks of my life were on the path. They wanted healing; they wanted to talk about healing. I could not escape.

I think every one of us does a sort of healing work almost daily. That may take the form of compassionate listening, setting boundaries or nurturing others. We do this in our relationships, our friendships, and our work lives. You may not get paid for it as a professional, yet you are doing healing work, the work of Life.

Think about it. Are you a healer for someone or for several friends or relatives in your life? For your associates at work, or your boss? How do you feel about it? Is it a burden? Do you want to help and just do not know how to stay clear? Do you not know how to avoid taking on and carrying their emotional baggage? Do you feel too vulnerable or too sensitive to help others?

In the next section I list ways to stay clear.

STAYING CLEAR

Staying clear is remaining free from anything that darkens or obscures your perceptions. When you are clear, you are heard and seen easily. You live life with a sense of certainty, without ambiguity. The best ways to stay clear are by:

- Grounding
- Releasing

- ◆ Boundaries
- ◆ Setting intentions
- ◆ Staying present

GROUNDING

Feel the earth below your feet. Stay in your body, here and now. Be in this moment, not in pain about the past or in fear about the future, but firmly rooted to embrace life. Grounding is easy for me. A large part of it is because my sun and moon astrological signs are in Capricorn, with Taurus as my rising sign. These three primary signs are all earth signs that are very grounding. Thank God!

I ground myself by getting off the concrete and making contact with the earth. I do this by going on hikes, lying on the beach, working in the garden, playing basketball, and riding mountain bikes, to name a few of my favorite activities. Being grounded is a natural state for me coming from a farm. I actually start to get restless and less clear when I am stuck in a high-rise building away from the earth.

I have a friend, Nancy, who is a writer. She lives in her head most of the time. She's a sweet person, very bright, and very intellectual. Every three or four months, like clockwork, she calls me in an emotional state of anxiety about lack of work or lack of relationship. It is a change from her intellectual state, and it makes her very uncomfortable. I remind her it is good she is feeling. Then I suggest she take a hike, or do something to get grounded. Recently she did a ceremony to acknowledge Mother Earth for her beauty, abundance, and resources. She sat under an oak tree, burned some sage, and did some breathing. She told me the anxiety just melted away, and she felt very clear after she got grounded. She also reported some hikers walked passed her as she was doing her ceremony. They asked to join her and she led her first Spiritual group experience. She was quite excited. I smiled at the subtle way Spirit works.

GROUNDING EXERCISE

Do something that makes you feel more grounded or connected to the earth. Go on a hike, walk around barefooted, go for a swim, make love, hold someone, eat root vegetables (carrots, beets, turnips, or potatoes), do yoga, or exercise.

When you are out of sync or feel nervous, emotional, spacey, or simply lousy, ask yourself, "Do I feel grounded?" The answer will probably be no. Be aware of when it is time to ground yourself, so you can heal and be in a place where you can help someone.

Ask Mother Earth for her support. I say the following affirmation: "Please help me ground myself, Mother Earth. Make me strong like the oak tree. Allow me to send energetic roots down into you. I am grounded. I am strong."

RELEASING

"Let go and let God." You may have heard this phrase—it is a good one. Release your past. Let go of the hurts, drop grudges, and forget blame. Forgive.

We have all been hurt, abused, and beaten down to some degree in our lives. What you choose to do with these experiences makes you successful, or unsuccessful, in the game of life. As you learned in the Personal Journey chapter, when you are able to release the past, let go, and forgive, the world is a far different and better place.

Ryan, a client in his forties, was facing marital problems and possibly a divorce. He was angry, and apparently, so was his wife. He was anchored in the blame game (she did this, she did that, etc.). In our work together I helped him release his anger and blame towards his wife. He held this energy in his shoulders, neck, and lower back muscles, energy that had been building up for a long time. As we were releasing this energy he got mad at me, thinking I was siding with his wife. I told him the anger was looking for a place to land as we released it, and it would not be me. I told him to give it up to God.

He called me shortly after to say that he finally got it—he had asked his wife for forgiveness and cried in her arms. By releasing her, the walls of resentment broke for both of them, and all the old toxins were let go. They were able to come back together in love. He said his wife was so relieved that he led the way to healing this time. It gave her more hope than she had had in a long time for their relationship.

RELEASING EXERCISE

Have you taken something on today? Some energy, an attitude, or some responsibility for another person? Are you feeling negative? Where do you need to release more in your life? From a new perspective, look at anything you may be holding. Release it! "Let go and let God."

Holding on to negative emotions and experiences affects your health and well-being. Holding negativity is the root of most disease and discomfort in the body. Effective releases, acceptance, and forgiveness can bring about physical healing, especially if they occur before the disease has destroyed the body's ability to heal. It is imperative to release and let go. You can begin by acknowledging and expressing gratitude. This will change your energy and empower your ability to release better than anything I know.

BOUNDARIES

The word "boundaries" was a big psychological buzzword in the 1990s and it is still widely used today. What are boundaries to you? Merriam-Webster defines a boundary as "something that fixes a limit or separating line." A limit or separating line is necessary for people and healthy relationships. We must establish boundaries to know who we are, otherwise we overlap and try to find identity through other people, and that becomes a time bomb waiting to go off. Clean and clearly communicated boundaries make for successful relationships. With well-defined boundaries, you will find it easier to stay clear. You must remain clear to do effective healing work for any extended period of time.

Being connected to your energy gives you the ability to have very clean boundaries. If you are in touch with your energy you will feel it when someone is crossing a boundary and sucking energy from you. Be aware of energetic boundaries.

BOUNDARIES EXERCISE

When someone close to you asks a question, try responding with a simple yes or no, without a long, drawn out explanation. See what happens. Do they keep digging to know why? Do you feel compelled to explain? Take a good look at the boundaries you have established with someone important in your life. It may not be easy to say no, or to say yes, for that matter. "Yes" often means "maybe," and "no" can mean "probably." Although working on boundaries may seem very difficult at first, once you get the hang of it, boundaries will give you freedom. And in this freedom lies an abundance of energy.

Jane, a forty-three-year-old mom, came to me complaining about her life. In particular, she felt her husband and 10-year-old son did not respect her. She said her husband degraded her and treated her like a servant, and she let him get away with it. Now, her son was doing the same. We quickly assessed the situation and got her to look at her boundaries.

Jane came in with what I call a "second-class" mentality. That is the way she felt about herself and other people just played right along. As long as she stayed second-class, she did not have to take responsibility for her life. She could wait, blame others, and rely on passive-aggressive excuses. This time, she was committed to take a stand for herself. She learned that she had to say "no" to her husband and son, and be willing to face the consequences. Once she started setting boundaries, she started experiencing amazing healings with her energy. Excitement returned to her life. The second-class act was gone. She gained respect for herself and it quickly followed from those around her, including her husband and son.

SET INTENTIONS

Setting intentions (goals) gives you a road map, a direction, a purpose. Having intention allows you to focus and to choose what you intend to happen. And, setting intentions puts the universe in motion to help you. Intentions alert your guides, your teachers, angels, and other helpers in life that you are on the move. When you commit to doing something, you start to believe in yourself. You develop more faith as you are guided and assisted by God. When you set intentions and take action, magic happens. Setting intentions is important for staying clear in both healing work and in life. I approach healing work and life in the same way, and intentions are a vital activating tool.

A Hollywood writer in his late thirties, Lance came to me with a complex situation. He had been hired to write a script by a big Hollywood production company and he was being paid big bucks for the top-notch project. Although a star director was attached, it was not someone Lance was keen on. I asked him who he wanted, and he said it did not really matter, because the producer wanted the star director. However, there was a certain person Lance wanted for this movie. He said that of course it would never happen, because this director was committed to several projects, etc. We worked with his energy, opened him up, and I asked him to see his "dream director" doing the movie. We focused intention on this happening. All positive events taking place, such as the attached director leaving the project because of another film he wanted to do. His dream director came on board, because his schedule magically opened up. The intention worked! I got a call about two weeks later and everything Lance intended was coming to fruition. He could not believe it. This story has had one of the most magical Hollywood endings that I have ever witnessed. He worked with the director for many months perfecting the story, and on the filming of the project. It was good for all of their careers. And I believe Lance's intention played a key role in its execution.

I literally use intention with most everything I do. Examples include:

+ Basketball: I visualize the game in my head before I play. I set intention around the team winning the game, and secondarily any points, rebounds, and free throws that I make.

+ Healing work: I set intention around how many clients I will see each week by writing down the total number the week before.

+ Healing retreats: I have everyone set intention verbally to initiate the work at the beginning of the workshop.

+ Writing this book: I set intention with each phase of its development such as completion schedules, feedback, and publishing decisions.

I set intention different ways, such as:

+ Visualizing it in my head in a meditative way

+ Writing it down

+ Speaking out loud to myself

+ Speaking out loud to a group

These are a few of the ways that work for me, but there are no rules for intention. The primary purpose is to figure out a Spiritual way to program yourself for success. I find that for myself, the best results come from a relaxed place of play and fun. I tailor each implementation of intention to the task at hand. Intention does not work with seriousness and rigidity. A relaxed sense of play lets energy flow and Spirit move around the truth of our destiny. Intention gives us a map.

SET INTENTIONS EXERCISE

Setting intentions can be approached like a game. Activate your imagination to draw out your inner child. With a specific situation in mind, determine what you want to happen, the steps to making it happen and how you feel about it; then, let go of the result. Approach the situation as if the desired result has already occurred. My point is this: make a choice about what you want to happen and set the universe in motion. Write it down. Speak it out loud. Play the game like a kid. Have fun. Set intention!

STAYING PRESENT

Staying present is part of being grounded and it deserves further mention. You must be here right now, in the moment, to heal yourself and to be an effective healer for others. If you are not present, you are somewhere else, unable to confront what you must confront, and unable to take responsibility for your life. You own your power when you are in the present. When you are not present, your power is easily given or taken away.

Jenny, a twenty-four-year-old actress, came to me with some issues I thought she should take to her acting coach. She explained that she was auditioning for big roles these days and was not doing her best. She felt like she could not stay present, that she would get nervous and leave her body. Her acting coach thought she needed some healing work.

I talked with her to get clear about what she was doing. We worked with her energy, clearing away the fear that was causing her to leave her body. She said she felt something in her belly. We looked into the energy and I had her describe it to me. She said it was cold and was a murky yellow color. I asked her if she had ever heard the term, "yellow-belly"? She said yes, and that it implied fear. We cleared the energy by bringing more awareness to it, and as we brought awareness to it, energy started to flow through the area. She connected to a childhood memory where a man tried to break into her bedroom window. Her mother heard him and called the police. Jenny said she remembered holding her breath and trying to hide as her mom freaked out, waiting for the police to come. She began to cry as she connected with the fear she had stuffed into her belly as a little girl. Then she started to laugh and get very excited as she realized the fear was leaving her body, that the fear was not her. It was something attached to her from a long time ago. The part of her Spirit pushed aside by the fear began to return. Her body heated up and started to vibrate. Then we worked at getting all this energy grounded so that she could stay present in her life. We set intentions with the auditions she had coming up, and she was able to stay present in every audition. She has been working steadily as an actress ever since.

We saw that Jenny was able to stay present and be in her own power after we released the trauma of something she experienced at a young age. Her energy led us right to the problem. Once we connected to the block, we were able to move energy through it by bringing awareness to it. As energy moved through the block, the memory of the event that placed it there revealed itself. Through this process, Jenny was able to realize that this energy from the past was making her feel small and unsafe, sabotaging her acting. When it was released out of her body her true self emerged, one full of laughter and joy.

STAYING PRESENT EXERCISE

Are you present? Do you spend a lot of time daydreaming? Do you avoid dealing with something in your life? Is it a fear of the future or pain from the past that keeps you from remaining present in your life? If you have fear or pain, work at staying in the present. Give it a try. Your power is in the present moment. Awareness that you are not in the present moment allows you to make a choice to get there.

STAYING CLEAR SUMMARY EXERCISE

Answer these questions:

• Do you stay clear and balanced in your life?

• Where and when do you get confused?

• Does confusion prevent you from dealing, confronting, or changing your life?

• What could you do and accomplish if you were clear in your life?

• Do you believe it is possible to be clear?

You have the opportunity to receive something valuable if you let this work sink in. A therapist friend once told me that her practice was built on people's misunderstandings of love, sex, and money. Her single clients are obsessed with looking for love and they have a fear of the lack of money; couples are falling apart, also because of sex and money problems. At first, I thought this was too simplistic, yet over the years I have found it to be true. Are you having problems in these areas? Dig deep and see if problems with love, sex, and money cause you to be unable to stay clear in your life.

Find your energy. Believe you can heal yourself and others. And, seek perfect clarity by grounding, releasing, setting boundaries and intentions, and staying in the present.

DOES LOVE MEAN I HAVE TO CARRY YOUR PAIN?

Must you carry your family's pain? Your ancestors' pain? How much of this energy is passed down through genetics and DNA? We may never know the answer, but we do know that the imprints around love are powerful. Thoughts, reactions, and behaviors are often passed from one generation to the next.

As people grow and become more conscious, this topic comes up. You may have found it easier to choose a partner who was less evolved than you, someone who needed a little fixing. Is he or she a "fixer-upper"? Many people see a person's potential, and marry the potential instead of the person. Ultimately, they know they are in wrong, unfulfilling relationships. They may complain incessantly, and never break free, lacking enough self-esteem to move on.

Why do people settle with love for less and think, "This is the best I can do?" Is it because life seems easier if someone is "less than," or is dependent upon you? Is dependency the same as love? Are you a parent to your mate? Has the sex dried up and now feels incestuous? Together for years, many couples are shut-down, miserable, resentful, and afraid to change, afraid to confront, afraid to grow or move on.

There are so many concessions around love, because people have not learned how to love and they do not know what love is. They respond to drama, abuse, control, and suppression as if it were love. This is an imprint from the past that is difficult to let go, an addiction to the negative and a hard thing about which to get clear.

In Los Angeles, an entertainment capital, I work with people who are in love with their mate's talent, not their person. When this happens, the relationship spins out of balance. Boundaries get blurred and the tests are intense. These relationships are destined to break down.

A 35-year-old production designer in the movie-making business, Laura, often fell in love with her directors; throw in an English accent and a few addictions, and she would be in head over heels. She was very talented and often commented about her addiction to troubled, yet talented individuals. She found them fascinating and far more exciting than "normal people." These infatuations generally lasted about three months with only one or two formal dates and the rest being drama, stalking, and other desperate measures for attention. In our work together, I have seen her grow and become more aware of her habits, although it is apparent that she is not ready to confront what a relationship entails. She is just not ready. I told her that when she hits forty, a "normal" relationship might start looking pretty good. I cannot fix Laura. She must implement the change herself.

We can be impaired with illusions about what love is, and unaware of how much work it is to nurture. Many books have been written about love, and they all come down to this: if you are not lifted up by another person's love, you may not have love. Love does not mean you must carry your partner's pain, fear, karma or baggage, nor must they carry yours.

As a healer, you must take care to avoid carrying other people's pain. You do not help them by taking on or transmuting their disease, unless you teach them how to clear and heal themselves.

Sensitive people may take on and carry other people's burdens without even knowing it. It is an empathic quality. And when you care about another person, it gets trickier, because the desire to help is so strong. The next thing you know, you are walking around with a headache or a stomachache, and the friend who just vented to you feels better.

The issues in this chapter are fascinating to explore. Much of my intention for this work is to help you get clear enough to choose what you want to experience around love. Remember, that if it does not lift you up, it may not be love.

IT'S NOT ABOUT ME

Healing work is not about me, and it is not about you, either. It is about something bigger, about getting out of our own way. When healing, I relax, open, and make contact with God. My faith then allows God to flow through me. God does the work.

As a double Capricorn (sun and moon astrological signs), I can be very willful, stubborn, determined, and focused—not all bad. These characteristics actually benefit me in positive ways. Yet, when I am more trusting and less willful, I become more in the present moment and I am better able to enjoy the process of life. I just open up and enjoy the ride. For example, when my daughter was born, I experienced a level of love and trust for the process of life that I had never felt before. It opened me up to the true miracle of life, and humbled me to the fact that much of life is not about me, nor about a need for me to be the center of my own universe. Children have a way of teaching us that life is about them!

"It's not about me" also means that healing work is not about fear-based negativity, or old thoughts I have bought into that in no way represent who I am today. Growth, change, and healing enable me to become more open. Now I am more accepting and less judgmental, easier on others and myself. In other words, most of the negative stuff that I originally thought was me, was not me at all. Negativity is not about me. If you can get out of your own way, God will show you the way.

EMOTIONS

Emotions are attributes that make humans truly unique creatures. As an actor, I studied emotions and the way they work. I use the words "emotions" and "feelings" interchangeably. Emotions give us a quality of expression on a human level much like how an artist uses paint. Another good description is that emotions are energy in motion. In other words, to emote is to move energy through your body and consciousness.

In the healing work, I look at the emotions as tools, not the be-all and end-all to the work, but simply a cog in the wheel. I use emotions to get to the truth and to get energy moving, yet I avoid being seduced into thinking they are the end result. For some people, just getting in touch with their feelings is a big accomplishment. For others, it can be a trap because they give total power to their emotions; essentially, their emotions run their lives. The key is to balance between the intellect and the emotions, with each governed by the heart. The intellect is in the head, the emotions are in the belly, and the heart is in between. It is important to get a handle on the power of emotions, that is why I talk about them again in this section.

I want you to connect with your truth as an emotional being. Are your emotions an asset to you as a human being, or are they a liability? Do you trust them to express yourself or do you deny them out of fear? Without emotions, life would not be the same. Perhaps we would cease to exist as a human race if we could not feel. We need emotions to be human. We need to feel. The intellect is not enough. Studies have shown that babies need to be held and nurtured. Orphaned babies who are just fed and left alone in their beds do not survive. Without an emotional connection or love and nurturing, humans do not thrive, heal, or live well. I believe in the value of our emotions to live, create, and express ourselves.

Yet, emotions can be crutches that keep us in a place of victimhood. Those who are led by their emotions respond to life like a yo-yo, depending on the person or thing that is pulling their string. They generally feel they are creative and that their talent comes from their feelings, and some of this may be true—nonetheless, I believe this limits their experiences and their ability to stay empowered.

When I tell people not to allow their emotions to run their life, there can be tremendous resistance and often very little application, because many people are emotional junkies. They love drama and the adrenaline rush the emotions provide. They think they would be boring if they were less emotional. I do not tell them not to feel; rather, I say, "Don't be controlled and dominated by your emotions."

> *George, fifty-one and self-employed, has a short fuse. Wherever he goes, a tornado of emotional fallout is sure to follow. Sooner or later, he has problems in most of his relationships. As much as I have been pushed to give up on George, I have not. I work with George to help him see how people respond to his energy.*

> *Born into a wealthy family, George has led a very privileged life and has been married four times. He is used to getting his way and he uses his emotions to test people. His experience with life is very dramatic. Always searching for the Spiritual connection outside of himself, I challenged him to lighten up and trust life more, and find Spirit within himself. The jury is still out on this man/child; I am a patient man, yet I am not sure he wants to be a responsible adult. At the end of the day I know I have done my job, bringing to his awareness the liability of the way he uses his emotions. Now it is up to him.*

> *A sixteen-year-old high school student named Lateisha also had a problem with her emotions. Everyone told her she was too emotional, and she was starting to believe them. Her mom thought she needed medication, although she was willing to hold off for healing and therapy. Lateisha had several breakdowns at school and it was touch and go with her parents. She was in the top of her class and was under tremendous pressure to excel at school; her parents wanted her to go to UC Berkeley as they had, and she did not want to disappoint them. We worked with her energy and cleared a huge amount of fear and anger. While she was mad at her parents for the pressure, she was still afraid to fail. I have seen her several times a year for the last six years, each time balancing her emotions. We called it a tune-up. She graduated from Berkeley recently, at the top of her class.*

This is not a male vs. female, Mars vs. Venus thing, although the emotional roller coaster is more applicable to women or to feminine energy in general. I do not define it that way, because I work with men (like George) who are very emotional and reactive in their lives, too. It takes a combination of male strength and female openness and strength to stay grounded as you deal with the intensity of your emotions.

When you suppress or deny your emotions, it is just a matter of time before a revolt happens, showing up as depression, aggression, obsession, possession, or even disease. Finding the right balance between the emotions and the intellect is a delicate matter, yet when balanced, these two elements are very powerful.

Why disease? When energy is blocked or held in the body, disease festers and the body starts to scream out. It begins with aches and pains, then with low energy and depression. Next are flu bugs and colds, compromised immune systems, anxiety, panic attacks and then physical ailments, such as ulcers, high blood pressure, arthritis, heart palpitations, or migraines. Many people begin the cycle of antidepressants, sleeping pills, and medications to ease the pain. Usually followed by more medication, this cycle continues and the body and mind suffer.

This psychological condition of over-emotionality may further deteriorate due to bad diet, high stress, lack of support, no Spiritual base, and having few tools available to change the condition. Even worse, there may be a total lack of awareness of the problem. Even with awareness, some people just give up hope that they can do something about it.

> At age twenty-nine, Lisa was facing an emotionally challenging time with a divorce. She went on a vacation and kept extending the trip to avoid going home and dealing with her life. After three weeks of avoiding the inevitable she came down with shingles, a painful viral condition related to chicken pox. The stress of avoiding confronting her life helped create this condition. Even an allopathic doctor told her it was stress-related.

The emotions that we try to shift in healing work are:

+ Anger

+ Sadness

+ Fear

And the emotions we work to enhance are:

+ Love

+ Joy

Every feeling is either a variation or combination of these five emotions. For example, gratitude could be a combination of Love and Joy, whereas depression could be a combination of Sadness and Anger. Depression could also be a variation of Sadness, and terror a variation of Fear.

To shift out of the three negative emotions, sometimes you acknowledge the emotion fully, and allow yourself to hit rock bottom with it. Other times, you must confront how you are using the negative to keep your life the same and to continue the cycle of victimhood and blame. Most of all, you must want to change your condition. Once you are clear about moving forward, the emotions shift. Where awareness goes, energy flows.

If this section is stirring things up for you, review the Pyramid Of Life section. Look at the four levels and evaluate the level upon which you are living your life. If you are stuck on a particular level, it may be a good thing, for at least you are now aware of it and you are acquiring tools to be able to change it. Also review the Personal Journey section.

FEAR VERSUS FAITH

"Fear versus Faith" was a topic at one of my healing retreats a few years ago. We are all familiar with fear, a negative habit to which we may become accustomed as we make life choices. Focusing on faith, rather than fear, is like a fork in the road providing us the opportunity to choose a different experience.

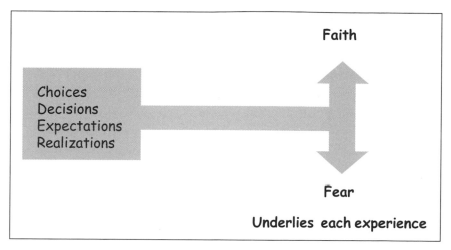

Figure 2. Fear versus Faith

One thing I learned at this retreat is that people are intimidated by the word "faith." They do not like to use the word. There are judgments that it pertains to a specific religion, or that it is some kind of New Age thing. I encouraged people to notice how many times per hour they feel or speak about fear as opposed to the times they feel or speak about faith. It is a staggering realization. Fear is the ingrained response for most people.

Faith comes from an intention to have a different experience; it is a choice to believe that the universe will support you when you take a risk and grow. Faith is a decision to take an action to change the course of your life, an expectation or confidence that everything will work out. Faith is realizing your choice to stay in the moment and enjoy the outcome, and to watch your garden grow.

The word "faith" is not necessarily of religious connotation. To me, faith comes from my belief in myself and is enhanced by my connection to God, Spirit and Nature. If I connect to red-tail hawks and this connection to them has a positive affect on my life, I will continue to use this connection to increase my faith.

Some people argue that faith comes from a direct connection to God. I agree with that too, but my point is that it all has to channel through me—even God. When I see God in everything and in me, I feel connected. I feel my faith.

I do not argue about God and faith. I believe that if a person is really connected to God, they have moved through much of their relationship with fear. The key words are "really connected to God."

Confront your fear so you can choose to have faith. Some examples are:

- To take risks

- To pursue your dreams

- To trust that the universe will support you abundantly

- To recognize healthy people with whom to have relationships

- To know it is safe to be in your body and no one will take away your power

- To believe it is safe to speak up

- To realize that the expression of anger is not going to get you killed, and that it can be a positive energy if channeled properly

- To believe you can have a healthy relationship with your family

MONEY

So many people are out of ethics, in fear, and terrified about money. They may be spending more than they are making or they may be holding on to every cent they make, depriving themselves of basic needs. Most millionaires that I know have been broke or bankrupt many times. Are they more or less fearful about making and losing money? Why is the average person insecure about their security with money?

Insecurity about money may be an inheritance of your family's views and experience regarding money. As much as you rebel and try to be free of those views, they are ingrained, especially the fear-based thoughts. My family's conservational ways are deeply rooted in my grandfather's memories of the Great Depression. He said, "You better work hard for a living. Money doesn't grow on trees. Kids today don't know the meaning of money. If you don't own your house and the land it's on, you're nothing. Don't get into debt." My family's views have made me conservative and responsible with money. I have worked hard to trust my ability to flow with the universe regarding money.

There are a lot of outdated myths about Spirituality, poverty, and money. You do not have to be poor to be Spiritual, nor do you need to give up all your worldly possessions to find God.

I have led some group workshops on the topic of money. In one of them, someone asked, "Why do you charge for Spiritual work?" I responded that healing work is my livelihood, and it is how I feed my family. As I have raised the value of what comes through me, the result of my work has become more precise, more valuable, and more in demand. This idea has been validated by people who voluntarily pay me extra money for my work, and who tell me that I should be charging more. For example, I was charging $100 per session several years ago, and people started giving me $150, saying I was the best bargain in town. As this happened I noticed the level of energy, awareness, and intuition also increased within the work. As I realized my value in doing this work, I started to trust the universe to support me even more. It is never about wealth. It is about a certain level of comfort within my acceptance to do God's work.

In the money workshop, I noticed the people who were the most stuck around their flow with money were those who had the most judgments about money. Some people felt money was bad. Others thought you could not want money and be Spiritual. Those who felt that money was a good kind of energy proved to have a better relationship with money. They trusted themselves to receive and distribute money, to use money to facilitate life, and to use it to help others.

My clients who feel victimized due to a perceived lack of money are those who get stuck on what they are asked to pay for healing. If I give them a free session, it seems there is no change or very little change, because I have bought into their views about themselves. When they pay for the work, they are able to commit to change and do anything to get it. It is about the exchange. If they are willing to work to receive healing, then they receive healing. If they place no value on themselves and want something for free, they are usually not able to receive.

Your views about money are indicative of your views of life. If you feel confident that the universe will support you abundantly, then you can embrace life. Can you learn this? Can you be led through your fears to embrace life? These are some of the questions I explore in my Spiritual work. How can I lead people to the Light? How can I enable people to step through fear and choose to experience something different?

Issues surrounding money are often excuses not to grow, to stay the same. When you are willing to risk moving out of the safety of what you know, you will realize that you have been living in a prison cell, and that you are set free when you take risks or leaps of faith. I am convinced that when you align yourself with your Spiritual Purpose, the universe will rally to support you. I ask people, "What do you need the money for? What are you supposed to do with it?" As they connect to their purpose and know why they are here, money issues become secondary.

Years ago I said to myself, "I am open to money flowing 360 degrees around and through me, no matter what the source, as long as it's positive." This was the beginning of my financial freedom. I opened to the universe supporting me abundantly.

In 1986 I made this statement as I left the corporate world. I left the security of two paychecks per month for something much less predictable and safe. I learned some good lessons about my relationship to money and about personal ethics with credit cards, especially when I ran up $15,000 in credit card debt. I snapped out of it and paid it off in less than a year and have not incurred credit card debt since. Eventually I made it to the healing work where checks are handed to me regularly and show up in the mail from phone sessions. I go to the mailbox with anticipation (of checks) rather than dread (of bills) these days.

THE WORK

After she made a trip home to Kentucky, my sister said, "Wouldn't life be so much easier if we had never started down this path? Look at our childhood friends—their lives seem more simple and happy. Maybe life would be a lot easier if we had stayed in Kentucky."

I responded, "Would Dorothy have been happier if she never left Kansas? Sometimes we are destined to change, to explore, and to lead. That's our destiny. There is no way to compare our life with childhood friends. Our destiny is different from theirs."

No one said Spirituality was easy or that it makes your life easier, yet it does enhance your ability to choose your experience in life. As your Spirituality increases, awareness increases, leading to higher consciousness and ultimately leading to calmness, contentment, peace, and love.

I am sold on healing and you are too, or else you would not be reading this. When you open to healing, you will experience it and will find yourself being led to more information about healing.

Before writing this book, all of my work came to me by referral or word of mouth without any sales work—no advertising is necessary for God's work. Occasionally, about five percent of the time, someone asks, "Exactly what do you do?" I laugh and say, "There is no answer that will satisfy that part of your brain." This is usually met with silence, and in that silence my intuition reveals what we need to work on. In a sentence or two, I tell the person what the problem may be; met with more silence, I then hear the question, "Are you talking about me, or everyone?" I say, "I'm talking about you." After an uncomfortable laugh, the questioning part of their brain starts to spin, and they quickly schedule an appointment.

This five percent prove to be very interesting. They are look-ing for answers with their heads, while I take them into experi-ences and let their brains catch up later. This process is the opposite of traditional therapy. Instead of going round and round with the brain and the ego, I activate energy centers and allow Spirit to shed light on the dark areas and flush out the stuck energy, false beliefs, and illusions held there. In a way, the brain gets neutralized. With the intellect removed from the pic-ture, the client lets go of the awareness that they know, and we venture into an expanded place where the senses are dramatical-ly increased. The brain catches up milliseconds later.

Traditional approaches taken in psychiatry and counseling serve a great purpose and there are great people in these fields. Nonetheless, traditional therapy can take years of circling the wagons around the brain and the ego. I believe that much of today's therapy work is outdated. Practitioners in these fields have told me that "talk therapy" is not working like it used to. Some clients have been in therapy and on antidepressants for years and the process is stalled.

Tim, a forty-year-old high school teacher, saw the same ther-apist for twelve years. He complained of feeling stuck in his life. I asked him, "Do you think you have done therapy?" The question irritated him. He had gone to twelve straight years of therapy once a week, with no breaks. I am sure he grew a lot from this experience, and it was not my job to evaluate that; it was my job to bring about change. He was stuck and some of it was due to his reliance on therapy. I encouraged him to ask the therapist for a break, which he did. I compli-mented him about the years of therapy that paved the way for rapid growth and expansion with our work, and left it open for him to return to therapy any time. I believe he knew all the information about what was wrong with him, yet he could not string it all together. As we worked with his energy, I witnessed some dramatic changes with Tim. He responded very passionately to energy and the opening of his heart. I saw him blossom in a short time because he was ready for some new experiences in his life.

Can Spiritual healing work for you even if you are not religious? Must you believe in God for it to work? Is this a religion or a cult? Healing does not have to be Spiritual in appearance for it to work. Personally, I find it nearly impossible to not be Spiritual with the work. Others connect in their own way. Even ardent atheists seem to have a strong connection to nature, and I use that connection to relate to them. I am not concerned that they use the name of God.

I do not care about a person's beliefs, I just want to find a way into their unconscious so that we can clear away the stuck energy. Therefore, this healing work is not based on a particular religion or belief system; it changes, based on the language needed to relate and connect to each person. I have no interest in taking away a person's personal power or controlling them. I want to empower them to be creative, strong individuals, so they can go out into the world and do their life's work. I want them to make a difference. This work is neither a religion nor a cult, but rather a deeply Spiritual process that helps connect a person to their higher essence.

A HEALING SESSION

To give you an idea of the framework of a typical healing session, I give you the following description that includes some of the technical things that may happen. Use your imagination to connect to the work and you will receive some free healing from this material, too. Where awareness goes, energy flows.

As my healing instincts and intuition develop over the years, I find that healing always occurs if I just speak my truth. The more I go with it, the more impact the work has. Over the years of using my gift, I have come to trust the gift as a muscle being strengthened.

A typical healing session lasts an hour or more, and is divided into two parts: Intellectual portion and emotional portion.

Table 1. Healing Session

INTELLECTUAL PORTION		
Length	**Interview/ Psychology**	**The Work**
5-15 Minutes	Talk and get acquainted. Ask questions. What does the client think is the problem? If applicable, catch up on the events you've been working on.	Watch client's energy. Watch environment. Be aware of everything (nature, sensations). Your higher self is communicating to the essence of the other person. Listen. Feel with your intuition. Get specific about a topic when directed by your intuition.

ENERGY PORTION		
Time	**Mechanics**	**The Work/Tools**
1-2 minutes	Client lies on their back on a massage table.	
	Start the two-stage pranayama yogic breath, consisting of two deep inhales and one exhale. Inhale through the mouth. First inhale fills the belly, second inhale fills the high chest. Then exhale though the mouth. At later stages the client can breathe through the nose.	The breath immediately starts the energy moving. Inhaling into belly connects to the emotions. Inhaling into high chest moves the emotions up the chakras, past the heart.

ENERGY PORTION (cont.)		
Time	**Mechanics**	**The Work/Tools**
1-2 minutes		Application of oils and use of other tools begins here. Refer to Tools section for additional information.
2-3 minutes (approx.)		Energy picks up. People either open or contract. The body gets very electrical.
5-7 minutes (approx.)		Endorphins kick in, relaxing the brain.
10 minutes (approx.)		Most people are fully into their experience, releasing stuck energy.
	Observe the body. See places where energy is stuck.	Work the area with sensitized pressure as well as use of other tools such as oils, sage, or sounds, bringing awareness to each spot so that energy can move through and heal it.
20-25 minute mark		The physical body getting clear.
30-35 minute mark		Return client to a normal breath pattern. Let client relax, recharge, and slip into a deep meditative state. Use tools such as the gong, sage, etc. to bring the work to completion.
45 minute mark		Allow person time to complete their process.

The breath work, or energy portion, is an ancient type of breathing practiced in the East for many centuries, similar to the "rebirthing" breath popular in this country in the 1970s. I added some variations; the intention behind the work is different as our society is in a different experiential place with energy these days.

Breathing through the mouth focuses awareness in the body, while breathing through the nose brings awareness to the intellect. For the healing process, breathing through the mouth stimulates energy and works the best. This is not hyperventilating, even though you are moving oxygen to the brain. The breathing is done in a controlled, meditative manner. The breath is a tool, not the "work" itself.

The breath relaxes you and gets you out of your head mentally. It starts energy moving by oxygenating the blood and working its way to the brain, stimulating the hypothalamus gland and other energy centers which release endorphins. As these endorphins are released, the connection to the body can become very heightened. Endorphins flow to the ductless glands (chakras) in the body and stimulate them. When energy moves, it is electrical. Generally, the emotions open and move freely when the endorphins are flowing.

As this is going on, I work with the client by dealing with their belief system around certain blocks or stuck places—this is where the "work" comes in. Our work is intuitive and, I believe, guided by a higher power. Yes, you can be trained to do this work! Your intuition is something that can be developed.

Ultimately, I fine-tune the energy so the person will feel their energy field and begin to work it themselves. When we find a block and focus on it, awareness goes to it and as this happens, the area expands, releases, and energy flows through. When this catharsis or cognition occurs, the person can let it go and become clear.

Truly amazing things happen when energy is moving. When energy moves, I feel Spirit move. I am more concerned with energy and Spirit than I am with emotions or intellect. If energy is really blocked and the person is stuck, it initially feels like hard work. Once the emotions engage and are released, everything moves easier. Breath, emotions, energy, Spirit—everything is connected. When a person is open, there is space for God to work, and a place for Spirit to move.

Rick, a thirty-eight-year-old high school basketball coach, came to see me because he was suffering from insomnia. His wife had been hoping he would try this work for a long time. The day he arrived for his session, he walked in and adamantly declared that he was not into this stuff, that it was his wife's thing. He said, "I am Western medicine all the way! She is the one who loves crystals and oils and sage. You're probably wasting your time with me." I laughed and agreed. He almost had me convinced. Then I remembered that God must have a plan here. I deflected the resistance by talking with him about basketball. After a while he relaxed, and I asked him about his insomnia. He said it was nothing and that he had just been having trouble sleeping. He started to close back down. When I mentioned the Lakers, he opened back up. I then asked if he wanted to try this work, and he said, "Will it help me meditate?" I explained the breath work to him, telling him it was an active meditation. He agreed to give it a try.

I got him started with the breath work. He struggled with his mind at first, then the breath took over and he started to feel his energy very quickly. I find this is the case with athletes; once we get them into the process they open very fast. The next thing I know he is whooping and hollering. He cannot believe he is feeling so much energy. His body is vibrating all over. Then, something comes up about his children and he becomes very emotional and starts to cry. He explains that he is worried about his children and feels bad about them not being in private school. It was the issue that was keeping him up at night.

All of a sudden he calmed down. Spirit came in and brought peace of mind to him about this issue. He went into a very deep state. When we finished he was ecstatic about his experience, though somewhat embarrassed by his emotions. I told him it was normal, and that most people experience the same thing. He was amazed. He left, and later sent his assistant coach to see me and told me that the principal and several teachers were also interested. He is even thinking about learning more about this work to bring it to his team. Apparently Phil Jackson, the Lakers coach who has brought a very spiritual approach to coaching and is one of the most successful coaches ever, is Rick's idol. Rick said, "If it works for Phil it might work for me."

I love this story because I got to witness a huge healing with this man. Rick said his deceased grandmother appeared to him in our session and assured him the children were fine in a public school, and for him to let go. Besides, they were in the school where he coached and he could keep an eye on them. He said it might take a while to get used to all of these changes, but he was now a believer. Rick realized that he had the power to meditate and could learn to bring it to his team, which I found very exciting.

I speak of Spirit. The word is derived from the Latin word *Spiritus*—breath, and *spinare*—breathe/to blow. Merriam-Webster defines the word "spirit" as follows: "1. An animating or vital principle held to give life to physical organisms; 2. A supernatural being or essence as a Holy Spirit; 3. Soul . . . "

Spirit moves like goose bumps through my body, especially up my spine and across my shoulders. This sensation is confirmed by nature within seconds when I hear or see red-tailed hawks or hummingbirds. Often, the wind will pick up at the same time. I work with Spirit, and I feel Spirit work with the client and myself. With Rick, Spirit moved as his emotions released; directly after that, he went into the deep state. That is when his grandmother appeared to him. He mentioned that his mind had a hard time allowing her to be there, but there was no way he was going to block her out. This session healed Rick's cynicism about Spirituality and healing. It opened him to more possibilities with himself, and others in his life.

As the person breathes and energy flows, several things usually occur. Energy begins to really pick up and he or she either opens or contracts. Opening is more fun! Whichever the case, the body gets very electrical, even with resistance. With resistance, more force is created to bring the opening, like using ten sticks of dynamite instead of one. When endorphins start to kick in, the brain is less and less in control. Of course, I walk them through the entire experience no matter how easy or difficult.

> *A sixty-eight-year-old retired schoolteacher named Carolyn came to me after being gifted a session by her son and daughter-in-law. I could tell she was there to appease them and really did not want to see me. I acknowledged that and asked her about being a teacher, and she softened up. I told her about the work and asked whether she would be interested or not. She finally relented, not wanting to disappoint the kids. While we gently worked with her energy, she was afraid. I persisted, and focused upward. Something came up about her students and the hundreds of stories she had collected from them over the years. Spirit showed up, and she got very mad about being emotional. I encouraged her to let go. She did and the floodgates opened. Thinking about her students touched her deeply, and she realized these stories needed to be made into a book. I was grateful she trusted me enough to let the truth come to her. She thanked me for not buying her "tough act."*

Many people take to a healing session like a fish to water and it is easy for both of us. When clients fully release their baggage, they may swear they are levitating. If we have been working with a lot of resistance, the physical experience within the body will be more intense in a restrictive way, and the body may go through temperature changes—usually cold to hot as fear is released. And, the body may tighten up in places where it is customary for that person to hold blockages.

For instance, mouths and/or lips may get tight and rigid. This is from not speaking up in their lives, holding back their voices. The hands may contract and appear arthritic, indicating a fear around love originating around the heart. This is called tetany, a mineral imbalance caused by increased oxygen flow; some people may get tetany, and some may not. This is where the holes in science start to show up for me.

> *When I worked with twenty-two-year-old Rob, a college senior majoring in computer technology, he started to experienced tremendous tightness around the mouth. He could barely talk. I had him scream, "It's safe for me to speak up!" He murmured at first until his mouth let go, his throat opened, and his jaw relaxed. He said he wore a mouthpiece at night, because he has been grinding his teeth since childhood. The "voice" said, "He is holding back his voice." I told this to Rob, and we worked deeper. He said he always wanted to be a Broadway singer, but his father would only pay for an education that meant something. Can you see the connection here? Once we broke though the blockage of not being able to express himself the way he desired, his true self emerged.*

Breakthroughs do not have to be loud and violent; they can also be peaceful and easy. It depends on the person and the level of resistance or fear. Rob may or may not go on to pursue a career in computers; for now, he has decided to give singing a try.

> *An RN in her fifties, Janet, came to see me complaining of arthritis and problems with her hands. We worked with her energy, and sure enough, as she was breathing, her hands started to lock up. I worked with the physical tightness in her hands to highlight the awareness in the fingers. Then we shifted our focus to the fear around her heart. As we cleared away this fear her hands magically opened and started to vibrate, pulse, and shake. They released so much energy that Janet felt the arthritis get significantly less right at that moment. We*

tracked the fear to the back of her heart where she held a belief that it was not safe to receive love. I asked about her father's heart. She said her father died of a massive heart attack several years earlier.

Her arthritis was a chronic condition, which showed up as her holding on to old hurts and pain around the heart, and feeling unloved. I have always believed the saying that states the hands are the extension of the heart. If the hands are blocked, it tells me a lot about a person's heart. Once we cleared this energy, Janet's hands got significantly better, and more importantly, her life got better. She realized she could open her heart and receive love.

Fear blocks a person's energy more than any other emotion. It is fascinating to me that people with the most physical resistance usually feel the most stuck in their lives and have the most difficulty letting go. They try to protect themselves, especially their heart. Fear can never protect the heart.

When I observe places on the body where energy is stuck, I may work on that area with sensitized pressure. Sometimes the slightest pressure can be painful because we are working energetically, not like a massage. When I am working energetically, energy tends to collect in the stuck place creating a massive traffic jam. The area may be knotted up like a charley horse or a sore muscle. I may need to just touch it, or say, "Relax your lower back." Bringing awareness to a particular spot enables energy to move through and heal it. I rarely need to use much physical force or pressure. I do not believe great healing needs to be accompanied by great pain.

As I see the physical body getting clear, I have the client return to a normal breath pattern. I tell them to relax and recharge their deep energetic batteries and they go into a deep meditative state. I continue to work around the body if needed. It may take a few minutes for the person to get it all back together.

My job is to be a scientist, to look deeper than the obvious. To be a Spiritual scientist goes beyond other ideals and techniques to find the truth. Observe and intuit everything, going to the core/cause of things. There are many levels to the sensitivity of this work. This book is about recognizing and developing your sensitivity to go to these different levels, so that your sensitivity can be used as a gift and tool for healing.

Some tools I use during a session may include touch, affirmations, oils, herbs, stones, crystals, or music. In the next section, my tools and their purposes are explained. It has taken me years to collect the various tools and to connect to their value. The tools vary, depending on the situation and the person. I bring intention to every tool I use—nothing is done to impress a client. My tools enable me to move energy, so that Spirit can do the work.

COUPLES WORK

After getting married and starting a family, I received more requests to work with couples. I like couples work because it is more complicated, and it can be interesting to work with the issues and interactions between two people.

I start out with the emotional history of the relationship, asking each partner to describe what is blocked or not working. While they talk, I watch the energy between them and see where they seem truly stuck. Then, I look beyond the physical and emotional to the Spiritual and explore why these two people are together and what they are working on karmically. I unearth their life issues and I assess where they are Spiritually, as well as, what they are ready to confront in their lives both as individuals and as partners. More specifically, I see what they mirror for each other. Many times, couples are too close to the forest to see the trees.

In our relationships, we choose a person most able to help us grow. On some level, the person we choose has the ability to bring about changes and growth in our consciousness. Many times people lose sight of the positive mirroring going on and start to see their partner as the problem in their life. It is not always the case, yet it is hard to step back from it if the negative is the strongest polarity between the two people.

My split-second intuitions have little to do with the story being told about what is wrong with the relationship. Besides listening to them talk, I am observing and listening to all the other signals and communications coming through from a higher plane. This takes a lot of work and concentration, and the trick is to not be drawn into the couple's drama.

After I hear the story from the couple, I lay them down to do the breath work together on the floor. I do the same work as I do with individuals. A unity usually occurs during the breath work and the stuck energy releases. Getting the stuck energy to move between the two and within each of them is the important thing. Spirit will orchestrate the healing if it is part of their destiny together.

Couples work is exhilarating, fun, and very rewarding, and at the same time, the universe takes the opportunity to teach me something about my own relationships. I make sure I do not miss the cosmic humor that comes with being a healer. It never fails that when I am healing others, the universe sends me mirrors to enable myself to get clear.

Married three years and with a newborn baby, Sid and Nancy came to me in dire straights. Among numerous strains on the relationship, Sid had thrown a bomb on the situation by volunteering information about an infidelity that took place earlier. Nancy was furious and about to throw in the towel. She was destroyed by the reoccurrence of childhood memories of her alcoholic father cheating on her mom. Sid and Nancy were at an impasse, with Sid trying to make amends and straighten things out and Nancy unable to forgive him. The baby motivated them to try to heal the relationship.

How could this situation be diffused? There were legitimate reasons for each to blame. Besides the infidelity, Nancy claimed Sid was mean and insensitive to her needs. He did not trust her with money and responsibility, and he did not help her enough with the baby. Sid claimed Nancy was often depressed and rarely felt sexual since they were married. She had misrepresented her credit card debt before they were married, creating a chain of unhealthy events to follow. Apparently they had discussed the possibility of Sid taking a lover during the time of his infidelity.

Problems, blame, he said, she said, their relationship was STUCK.

I looked at these two good, creative, artistic people. I could tell they were both a lot of fun, yet they had each other pinned to the wall. How could we start the healing process with forgiveness so far away?

I asked them why they thought they came together. Unsure, they believed their child was the prominent reason. We worked from that point, setting their love free for the benefit of the child. We looked at their options, and I would like to report a happy ending, but this relationship ended in divorce. They decided that they both needed time and distance before healing could occur. They both took the intense lessons from our short time together and started to reconstruct their lives.

Sid and Nancy have lived up to their word about their child, who is a truly exceptional being getting quality love from both parents. I think he is better off with his parents' divorce. At least now he is in a positive environment in two households, rather than in a state of tension and difficulty in one. As his parents make room for healing and forgiveness with each other, they will be able to move on to healthier new relationships.

Alice and Dan were a young professional couple who came to me as they were just getting together. I had worked with Alice a few times before and she wanted to set intention with Dan about their relationship. She had a feeling about this one. Dan had not done much Spiritual work, but he adored Alice. They were up front, honest people. We set intention, worked with their energy as a couple, and connected them through their hearts. It was a beautiful thing. They committed to always communicating and being open with each other, and also agreed to honor the other's request for outside help if needed. They married a short time later. I usually see them a few times a year together or separately for a tune-up. Their love is evident and infuses the relationship. I enjoy working with couples that embrace the opportunities, as well as challenges, to learn and grow together. I describe Alice and Dan to other couples, for they exemplify a way of being together that flows from contentment and peace within themselves as individuals.

Alice and Dan are not better people than Sid and Nancy, they just have a different walk along their Spiritual paths. Sid and Nancy came together to work some things out with each other, together or individually. Alice and Dan came together to do some things with each other and within themselves. Alice and Dan may have a more desirable existence, and I have a lot of faith in their future. I know Sid and Nancy will work through some of their issues with each other, and I foresee great healing for them. I am a patient man.

CHAPTER FOUR

TOOLS

In healing work, the tools that I use have various, distinct uses. They can be broken down into the following two groups:

- Tools used to heal others

- Tools used to heal yourself

I list the tools in a relative order of use and importance, and the order will vary on a case-by-case basis. Some of the information presented in the following table may seem repetitive, however the intention is to distinguish the use of each tool separately. While you incorporate most of the tools into the practice of healing others, take care to set aside specific tools, time, space, and intention to care for yourself. This will enable you to remain clear and be a more effective conduit for God to do his work through you.

TOOL DESCRIPTIONS

The following are descriptions of how each tool may be used. For now, do not get too caught up in the difference between clearing and grounding—it is a fine line. My definition

Table 2. Tools Chart

Tools	Primary Use	Heal Others	Heal Self
The Breath	clearing/grounding	X	X
Essential Oils	clearing/grounding	X	X
Sage	clearing	X	X
Cleanse Spray	clearing	X	X
Buffy Connection	grounding	X	X
Native American Medicine - Spirit	clearing	X	X
Stones for Balancing (Boji and Ocean)	grounding	X	X
Affirmations/Clairaudience	clearing	X	X
Music	clearing/grounding	X	X
Gong	clearing	X	
Sweet Grass	clearing	X	X
Juniper	clearing	X	X
Collage	grounding	X	X
Clean Space	clearing	X	X
Didgeridoo	clearing	X	
Dream Work	clearing/grounding	X	X
Eye Pillow	grounding	X	
Pau Santo Wood	clearing	X	X
Incense	clearing	X	
Ozone	clearing	X	X
Native American Shields	grounding	X	X
Cleanses	clearing/grounding		X
Health/Exercise	grounding		X
Rose Quartz	clearing		X
Bodywork	clearing/grounding		X
Prayer	clearing/grounding	X	X
Family	clearing/grounding	X	X
Full Moon	clearing	X	X
Tool Cleansing Techniques	clearing	X	X

for clear/clearing is as follows: free from anything that darkens, able to be seen through, pure in color, easily heard, completely certain, no confusion, and no guilt. Ground/grounding is to connect to the earth, or to have training in, or knowledge of, the basics of something.

THE BREATH

Breathing is the primary tool to get the process of healing work started; plus, it's cheap, it works, and is better than any drug or stimulant. Nonetheless, the breath is not the totality of the work. But it is worth further mentioning here. If anything, it is an active meditation that creates a space in a person's intellect to enable you to work deeply to their core. Breathing allows you to go to the depths of the feelings and into the subconscious.

As the breath stimulates energy in the body, the healer's job is to focus awareness into areas where the person is stuck, generally correlating to areas where their energy is stuck. The breath moves energy to those areas, right against the blocks. The energy from the breathing process raises the vibration by stimulating the hypothalamus gland (crown chakra) and then the body's lower charkas; the hypothalamus releases endorphins, which have a very high vibration. This vibration is an electrical current that moves through the nervous system and hits against the block. The block is usually fear or some sort of resistance stopping the energy flow. The breath keeps pressing energy against the block and this is where things get very intense. With some people, continuing with the breath pushes energy through the block and they open up; more specifically, they open their hearts as energy turns to Spirit when the healing occurs. Others who are caused discomfort from the breath will try slowing the breath and giving in to the familiarity or comfort of the resistance. Both approaches bring awareness to the body, to the subconscious, the intellect, the emotions, and to the person. The most desired outcome is when the person opens up and releases the block. Powerful healing can also occur as the person gives in to the resistance. The outcome is slower, yet eventually the healing has a chance to occur. The key is to get awareness into a person's conscious mind so that they can understand there is a block affecting their reality. The length of time it takes to change their reality is their own choice. As a healer you cannot force-feed anyone.

The breath moves energy quickly, and a focused awareness ultimately clears the block. The healer helps to focus this awareness. Once the energy has moved, the breath can be shifted to another style, such as long, deep breathing through the nose. This can reduce the energy flow to a more pleasant meditative level.

Tell your client to move slowly when you have completed the process. Once the person sits up, he or she will usually feel a little drunk for a few minutes. This happens because we are creating an expanded reality through the endorphin release process, as well as freedom of expression through the emotions and the chakras. It is always powerful to release endorphins consciously, and that gets greatly enhanced because of the breath.

> *A thirty-year-old client named Rikki described her process as the most intense experience of her life. She said it was ten years of therapy rolled into one session. However, I believe there was an alignment that happened in the timing of us getting together. All of her previous work prepared her for our deep cleanse and release. The breath was the fuel that facilitated the combustion. Then Spirit stepped in and did the rest of the healing by bringing clarity to her about her life.*

The act of breathing the two-stage breath releases endorphins that are normally liberated when we are afraid. In a healing situation, endorphins are released in conjunction with a positive emotional experience. The breath is the fuel that powers the work to bypass the intellect, enabling people to break through the control or psychology of their mind.

Your clients will want to stay in control of their minds because they fear the unknown. The breath helps release this fear. Oxygen is the stimulant that sparks the endorphin release, a key to the work that keeps people coming back for more.

At age eleven, Harlan was a serious young man who came to see me because his mom was concerned about his tension and stress. She said he had the worries of an older man. As I talked with Harlan, he was nervous, and nothing much came out of the dialogue. Once we started breathing he quickly began opening up. After fifteen minutes I had his mother come in and join us. He was amazed that he could feel himself vibrating all over. I had him repeat some things he had told me about his mom and dad; they had been fighting recently and had talked of separating. He was extremely upset and had not communicated this to anyone. When he revealed this to his mom, he broke down and started weeping, and his mom quickly joined him. I was quite moved.

When the vibration gets to a certain level and the right awareness is brought to a block, a fear, or stuck energy, catharsis happens. The truth comes out, and you do not have to analyze it to death; the answers simply come with the release of energy and/or the emotions. Even though this can be done without the breath, I find the breath is the expediter and acts as a truth serum. The breath is powerful and freeing at the same time. Harlan did not have predispositions about the breath or the healing work. He did not know he had blocked emotions and energy, but when he sat up, he asked his mom to do it again.

Essential Oils

I am committed to the use of essential oils in the healing work. The oils I use carry a specific vibration that is clear and consistent over time. They smell great and they change the energy of a person instantly. Yes, I am talking about aromatherapy, which is the use of oils extracted from plants to alleviate physical and psychological disorders, usually through massage or inhalation. And I am talking about much more than healing through smell. These oils have a distinct electrical frequency that shifts a person's energy when it comes into contact with their senses. I am talking about the power of the essence and soul of a plant. Essential aromatic oils are the true pharmacy of nature. I have specific uses for many of the oils. With a bit of research and some practical application, you will come to understand how essential oils will aid in your work.

There is one story involving a client named Dennis that sums up how I feel about the use of aromatherapy oils. Dennis was a clothing designer going through a rough time. As we worked, I noticed his deep response to the oils I was using. The work went very deep and the session was quite magical. When I saw him one week later, he reported that he had never felt better. He wanted to know more about the oils; he told me he had refused to bathe for three days after the work, not wanting to wash away their faint scent. The smell reminded him of the power of the work, and that sustaining the feeling was more important than a shower. I have heard this same story from many people. I am very careful in the application of the oils so as to not get them on people's clothes, although inevitably some oils may make contact with the clothing. Clients sometimes wear the same shirt for several days because of the lingering smell, and refuse to wash it during this time. It tickles me to hear these stories, because in some small way it shows me how important it is for people to heal, and the degree they go to in order to sustain a connection to being healed. The oils play an important role in this process.

Here are the oils I use regularly:

Grounding Blend

This oil is a blend I use for grounding a person's energy. I use it on the arches of a client's feet to open the electrical system in the body and to start to ground his or her energy. I suggest using it at the beginning of a session. It smells good and has a distinct ability to facilitate energy work. When you apply the oil, have your client say, "It is safe to be in my body. No one is going to come and take my power away."

Steven, a fifty-year-old fireman, informed me as I applied this blend to his feet that he was starting to feel something moving in his body. Was that energy? He said he was a little uncomfortable being touched by another man. Eventually he relaxed and had an amazing session. He commented that the smell of the first oil (Grounding) really opened him up and got him to relax. The smell reminded him of a time in his childhood when he played a lot in the woods. As these memories moved through him, he realized he was definitely feeling his energy. Before we had worked, he said he was not sure if he knew what his energy felt like. Grounding facilitated connecting him to his body and emotions as the breath raised the vibration of his energy.

Open Heart Blend

This oil is a blend of great-smelling oils with rose as the centerpiece. Use this oil on the heart chakra to "jump-start" the heart and help it open energetically. Virtually every woman who smells this oil falls in love with it, perhaps due to the rose scent.

Judy, a dancer, stopped me as I applied this oil. She said, "What is that smell?" I told her it was an oil called Open Heart. She said she wanted to get some. It is a common reaction to Open Heart, a beautiful blend of fragrant, appealing oils. Anything that can get a person to open their heart by just smelling must be special.

Frankincense

Use frankincense oil on the third eye. When you apply this oil, have your client say, "I can't figure everything out." This affirmation helps to relax the forehead and third eye area. I use this oil as an initiation type of oil on the third eye and crown chakra. Frankincense is an expensive oil but is worth every penny, and it has proven to be one of my favorites. It has a magically strong, sacred smell and property. I understand why it was valued like gold in ancient times and still is today. I think much of that was due to its power as an anointing oil.

Carl, a fifty-two-year-old nurse, described frankincense as a fragrance that hit him strongly; he did not like it at first, but he found himself yearning to smell it again. The oil did something to him. He said it startled him every time he smelled it, and then it transported him somewhere deep in his subconscious. Carl liked the journey. He quickly realized frankincense was a healing oil for him.

A thirty-four-year-old writer named Tracy had an interesting experience with frankincense. I put a drop of oil and a meteor stone on her third eye and she immediately started to see her aura. She was seeing colors around and inside her body. She could feel her third eye spinning and it heated up so much that it felt like it was burning. I had used frankincense and the same meteor on her many times before without any reaction or opening like this. In addition, we were doing the deepest healing work yet with her and we both agreed it was the combination of the scent, the stone, and the work coming together that facilitated this experience. It was very powerful and I believe the frankincense contributed greatly to this experience.

Sandalwood

Use this pure oil on the solar plexus for the third chakra. When applying the oil, make circular motions and pull the energy down towards the belly. Tell the client to release any people they are in a tug-of-war within the solar plexus, to let go of any will-centered battles.

Sandalwood is another ancient oil used often today as incense. I like the aroma of this oil and I use it on myself from time to time.

One client, Kerry, commented that sandalwood stimulated her in ways that always took her back to her mom. She thought her mom wore it when she was younger. When Kerry smelled it she would start to get emotional about the difficulty she had with her mom, almost in competition for her father's attention. Sandalwood provided us with a way into areas where Kerry was stuck.

Peppermint

Use peppermint oil on the belly and lower back areas for the second and third charkas, especially when you see bloating in the stomach or energy stuck in the lower back. The peppermint smells great and has a nice, warm, penetrating action that soothes the belly and helps digestion. Be careful with this oil, as it is very hot and can sting sensitive areas such as the eyes.

Molly, in her thirties, had suffered from constipation and bloating for many years. The first time I used peppermint on her belly the penetration of the oil assisted us in clearing some very blocked emotional energy. Over time, our work helped with Molly's constipation and peppermint oil contributed to the healing by stimulating energy to move in this region.

Clary Sage

Use clary sage oil on a woman's lower belly, lower back, and ovary area. Clary sage grounds the energy around the ovaries and helps to balance the first and second chakras. A little of this powerful oil goes a long way. This is another oil with a very strong, distinct odor, though it has a tendency to grow on you over time.

Betty hated the smell of clary sage the first time she smelled it. Like Carl with frankincense, she said it nauseated her. I explained that was a healthy response and the oil could prove to be an ally in the future. The stronger your repulsion to the oil, the more it has to offer you. This proved to be true as we worked longer together. Betty grew to love clary sage, and expressed a feeling of being more grounded and creative through opening the first and second chakras.

Lavender

Lavender oil can be massaged deeply into the throat and the back of the neck, particularly when a person is having trouble breathing or experiences tightness in the upper chest. The scent of this oil soothes and opens the throat or fifth chakra. Lavender is a general all-purpose oil to be used anywhere on the body with fairly good results. If you had to choose one oil, this would probably be the best choice for its versatility.

A stressed-out entrepreneur, Ron grew to love lavender as he found its relaxing, soothing properties. A perpetual insomniac, he found he could put two drops of lavender on his pillow at night and sleep like a baby. His wife stocked up on lavender when she saw how it worked, and attributed it with saving their marriage.

SPRAYS

Use the forthcoming oils as sprays. In a spray bottle, use one drop of oil per ounce of purified water.

Cleanse Blend

This oil is a blend used to cleanse and purify a space or a person's aura. I rarely use the oil undiluted—I love it as a spray and use it constantly. It clears my space and the air of energy that needs to move on, and also clears microbes such as viruses, bacteria, fungus, and other critters, including spider mites. This is definitely an essential oil.

A schoolteacher was sitting next to me on an airplane when I broke out my spray bottle and misted myself several times during a flu-ridden, Christmas-season flight. She asked if I would spray her. She said that it smelled so good she did not care what it was. I told her I was using it to cleanse the air around me. The next thing I knew, I had a conversation going with other passengers. Everyone was concerned about the air quality on this ride. My little spray bottle stayed busy the rest of the flight.

AROMATHERAPY

(Smell Only)

OPENS THE 7TH CHAKRA
Blue Lotus

OPENS THE 4TH CHAKRA
Rose

OPENS THE 2ND CHAKRA
Jasmine

OILS

(Applied to the Body)

7TH CHAKRA (CROWN) AND
6TH CHAKRA (THIRD EYE)
Frankincense

5TH CHAKRA (THROAT)
Lavender

4TH CHAKRA (HEART)
Open Heart

3RD CHAKRA (SOLAR PLEXUS)
Sandalwood

2ND CHAKRA (PELVIS, OVARIES,
CENTER OF LOW BACK)
Clary Sage
Peppermint

*Peppermint and Clary Sage overlap
some of the same areas

1ST CHAKRA (ROOT)
Spikenard *(top of feet)*
Grounded *(arches of feet)*

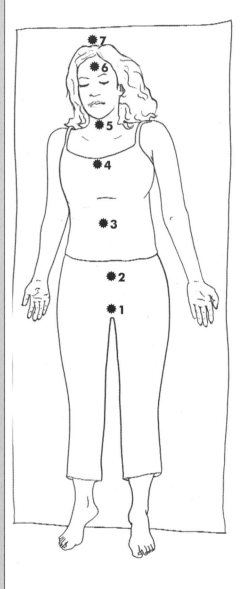

Figure 3. Application of Essential Oils

Manifestation Blend

I love this oil, which is a blend of oils used for manifestation. I use it constantly as a spray. I keep a bottle on my desk and spray myself several times a day, misting my head, neck, and shoulders.

> *A massage therapist named Gary came to me with severe financial issues. We worked with his energy and cleared all the physical and energetic blocks in his lower back pertaining to money. We cleared his belief system of feelings of lack of support, and I sent him home with a spray bottle of this oil, which he started using with good results. His financial picture started getting better. He said he sprays himself several times a day with this oil. He also sprays his apartment, especially the living room, and even his cats and dogs (which he figured out on his own.)*

Lavender

Lavender is very soothing when used as a spray, and the oil may also be diffused. Diffusing lavender oil into your healing space helps to keep it clear, peaceful, and relaxing.

DIFFUSER

An invaluable tool for clearing a space, a diffuser is a machine that pumps air through oil and distributes a fine mist into the air, a process that quickly clears a room. Unlike a candle diffuser that heats the oils, this machine does not change the properties of the oils. You can use a timer to activate the diffuser for a few minutes every day.

Check my website at www.thereluctanthealer.com for more information about oils and other tools mentioned in this section.

Sage

Sage is a sacred plant. I use it to clear energy, and to purify and change the energy in a room. I pick my own sage to connect with its growth in the wild. In my ceremony with sage, I thank the herb for its help in healing.

I am a firm believer in the sacredness and cleansing power of white California mountain sage. Although there are other wonderful sages that grow around the world, the one that speaks strongest to me is this white sage that grows in the mountains around Southern California. Over the years, I have located a few patches from which I take a picking once a year, usually in the fall. I ask permission to pick some of the sage and if it is a dry season I bring some extra water to share with the plant. I discovered this sage one night while driving in the mountains. Noticing a plant glowing in the night, I pulled over and discovered some gorgeous sage plants. This was very exciting because this sage has worked wonders in my healing practice. I usually burn one leaf per person, so a little goes a long way. I rarely bundle sage up and burn it as a smudge stick. I find that smudging, which is to direct the smoke around the body with a feather or with several feathers, wastes too much of the plant and may have more of a burned smell from lighting and re-lighting it. Lastly, sage can mold slightly as it is tied together green in bundles. This plant is a precious resource for me, so I value it one leaf at a time.

There are several aspects to the power of sage besides clearing. It has soothing properties when burned around most people. If there is a negative reaction to the pungent smell of sage, the client may well need clearing with sage. Eventually, these people grow to love the smell of it. My dog Buffy used to hate the smell of sage and would run away from it. Now, she enjoys having sage burned around her.

White sage is good for nerve damage and numbness from surgery or an accident. When I burn it around a client's feet, they often feel the return of feeling as an electrical shock. I cannot explain it. I figure the Spirit of the sage plant is doing something.

Louis, a fifty-year-old dentist, heard about my healing work and he had just experienced major back surgery for scoliosis. After they put him back together, his feet were about ten degrees different in temperature. The right foot was hot and the left one was cold. He wondered whether this was permanent and I told him I did not know; apparently neither did his doctor. There were other issues too, so we did our work together clearing his body and I kept my eye on his feet. After I got Louis balanced and relaxed with the breathing, I burned sage around the soles of his feet with the smoke rolling gently over them. All of a sudden he dramatically leaped into the air about twelve inches off the table. He said, "What did you do? I got shocked!" I was surprised and I told him I was just burning sage around his feet. I touched his feet and they were vibrating and coming into balance. I could feel the energy regulating itself and in a short time they were the same temperature. Although there is no scientific explanation for this, I know the power of sage. It has proven itself to me many times. It is one of the strongest purifying healing plants/tools I use.

I simply love the energy and smell of sage, whether fresh, dried, burned, or used as an oil. And, I can truthfully say that I have seen people from around the world respond very strongly to the smell and to the clearing properties of sage.

BUFFY

As I mentioned earlier, I grew up with animals on a farm. I love them almost as much as I love people.

I have a wonderful, sensitive, beautiful dog named Buffy. A basenji mix, she is cat-like, clean, and curious. She looks like a little deer with big pointed ears. She weighs around thirty pounds even though she eats like a Saint Bernard.

She has been with me since 1991, when someone dumped her at my friend Donna's house, and the friend eventually persuaded me to keep her. I did not want the responsibility of a dog at that time because I was living in Burbank in a duplex apartment without a fence. However, it turned out to be one of the best things I was ever persuaded to do in my life. Buffy has been one of my most treasured companions. She has taught me more about loyalty and unconditional love than any other relationship. I thank Donna for the gift of companionship that Buffy has given to me.

Figure 4. Buffy

I have friends with parrots, cats, snakes, horses, ferrets, cows, and pigs. These animals bring so much to their owners. They give us good training for parenthood because they teach us about dependency and responsibility. Buffy has certainly done that for me.

You do not need to have a dog or a pet to be a healer, although animals do add a level of sensitivity to the work. They bring their instinct and awareness to every situation. However, pets can also be a distraction if you do not have a good connection with them. Buffy has a good grounding quality for people who are nervous. She also helps me keep an eye on the surrounding environment, alerting me when nature is communicating, i.e. when another animal is close by, and announcing when a client arrives.

I began healing work right after she came to me. Sometimes I think she believes herself to be the healer. She insists on being present at all the healing sessions and groups. If she misses something she gets upset, so I let her participate in virtually all of the healing work. The only time she misses out is when I travel.

She generally greets clients at the front door with a few barks, and smells them to see where they have been and to take inventory of their animals. She is particularly interested in other "dog people," especially people with several dogs. After greeting the guest, she retreats to her bed in the healing room, unless she wants to stay connected to the person a little while longer for some petting.

As I work with the client on the table, Buffy sleeps deeply, often snoring. When I decide the session is about to wind down, she wakes up without me saying anything. When the client begins to get up, Buffy greets them again, usually with more affection and persistence, as if she wants to physically connect with the energy the person has experienced, possibly helping to ground it. Buffy and my clients usually experience a very loving connection. If Buffy is not in the room, my clients will ask, "Where is your dog?"

Several years ago, I realized she was doing something else for me. Some clients said they had dreamed of Buffy, or that she had come to them in their dreams. I realized they were traveling to see me in their sleep on the astral plane, and they would be coming for more energy work or help from me. Buffy was intercepting them so I could get some rest. They remembered Buffy in their dreams. It made so much sense to me.

Sleeping curled up in her bed beside mine, Buffy is a true guardian. I am grateful to have her watching out for me, covering my back. She truly is my best friend.

Sacred Things/Altar

My healing altar holds sacred things that I use to heal and for Spirit. By sacred things, I mean objects that hold special meaning to me; these objects do not necessarily have any religious connotations.

My altar currently consists of a piece of cloth, an old, tattered textile from Peru. This is an important piece because it holds everything together and gives my altar form. Many things may work as the base cloth or container of your altar, such as a bandana, scarf, towel, rabbit skin or deer skin—it is your choice. The sacred things on my altar include:

- Four picture cards of Archangels Michael, Raphael, Uriel, and Gabriel

- Four prized stones that I sometimes allow people to hold

- Two hand-painted hummingbirds

- Two turkey feathers

- An abalone shell filled with sage

- A clam shell with pau santo wood in it, also called "holy wood"

- Three crystals

- A piece of pink-colored rose quartz

Figure 5. Altar

I use the stones, crystals, feathers, sage, abalone shell, and pau santo wood for clearing in my healing work. Other altar items hold space for me to anchor or ground, such as the images of the archangels and the hummingbirds. I move things around and change the flow of the energy on my altar and healing space quite often. I also cleanse and purify many of the items during the full moon, every few months.

My altar is casual and does not look too serious. It is my anchor or grounding point, and I like it. I look at it as an expansion of beauty, an artistic expression of objects that are sacred to me, and an expression of what I consider to be my medicine, things that Spirit has sent to me. I tend to be organized about my belongings. Everything has its place, and the same goes for my altar.

When I look at my surroundings, I see altars everywhere: my bookshelves are altars for my books; my desk is an altar for my communication tools—the phone, computer, fax and printer.

ALTAR EXERCISE

Look around your space and notice where you have altars, such as a fireplace mantle or the top of a bureau. What do they say to you? Can they be arranged in a way that feels fresher and more alive? Do you have some things tucked away in a drawer that hold special meaning to you? What would happen if you placed them out on display, with intention? See if you can create altars that are healing and sacred to you.

NATIVE AMERICAN MEDICINE

Although I am not an American Indian, I do honor their customs. Native American traditions resonate with me, at least those I know about and understand. The culture just seems to be in my bones. I consider myself a novice to their teachings and ways, though I grew up in a territory in western Kentucky (Kantuck-Kee) known as the sacred hunting ground of the Shawnee tribe. One of our farms was an Indian village and many artifacts were found there. My father found many arrowheads and grinding stones on the highest hill overlooking the surrounding valleys. Because the artifacts were found there, we realized this was the site of the camp.

I feel and connect to earth and nature like the American Indian. I have described to you my powerful connection to red-tailed hawks—I feel a strong connection to Spirit through the hawks and through all of nature.

Several years ago I was given a medicine shield from my friend Michael. I did not know what it was at that time. I thought it looked nice and that I should accept it out of respect. I did not relate to it much at first, but I later learned that a medicine shield reflects an individual's medicine. It can be associated with healing power, protection in battle, success in hunts, and guidance in dreams or visions. The shields are circular, representing a never-ending cycle of life, death, and rebirth, much like the circular medicine wheel, consisting of stones laid on the land. There is much meaning and symbology to the circle in Native American medicine and the shield is one of them.

I have added to the medicine shield over the years, bringing it into my own reality, and have felt it grow in power. I have added many feathers, pieces of animal hides, plants, minerals, and some select pieces of jewelry. The shield is a treasured expression of my faith in the world of nature in the Native American way. I have much respect and humbleness towards these traditions because they are based on connecting and participating with everything in nature. Long live the indigenous people of Mother Earth!

I long to live on open land again to better commune with nature. Since being removed from the farm for many years, I feel the land calling me back. Now it is time to find a piece of land that I can steward. I cannot really possess land, even if I own title to it. If Mother Earth wants to claim it for herself, or wants to make a statement about modern humanity's abuse of the earth, she will. I will ask permission to be a protector of the land, rather than a controller of it. I look forward to the day when I will purchase the right to be the steward of a special piece of magical Mother Earth. I am now moving into the manifestation phase to have the "right" piece of property attract me to it. I understand the way the native people looked to the land, with honor and respect, and I do the same. I will encourage all of nature to reside on the land—all will have a home there.

Perhaps I've strayed from the topic of Native American medicine by talking about property, but land is vitally important to me, and many people will feel likewise in the future. A piece of land will be home to the Creative Healing Art (heart) Center, which will be home to all facets of my healing work. The center and the land will serve as models in nature, in the world of this healing work.

To obtain the benefits and the elements of Native Medicine in the healing work, I pay close attention to nature every moment of my life. I watch for every sign, even when multitudes of man-made distractions rise around me. I trust nature. I watch daily for hawks, hummingbirds, butterflies, and crows. Among the physical tools I use are sage, sweet grass, juniper, cedar, bird feathers, and a medicine shield for clearing and grounding in the work. My life is an awareness zone, even when I am not working. Native Medicine is a barometer in my bones. Now, you need not be like me to do healing work. My interest in Native Medicine is part of my trademark, my stamp. Yours may be different.

CLEAN SPACE/CLEAN AIR

When energy flows well in a space, healing work comes easier. One way to improve the flow of energy is to keep your space immaculately clean; that is, the carpet should be vacuumed every day to avoid dust, dirt, and cobwebs. I find a clean space very clearing.

Air quality affects energy flow. In addition to diffusing oils in the air, which help to keep the air clean, clear, and smelling great, you can use an Aranizer. This is an ionizer that releases negative ions into the air. The Aranizer removes impurities and adds ozone to the air. Run it for a few minutes at the beginning and at the end of the day. If the air gets stagnant during a session, turn the Aranizer on for a few minutes to clear energy that is stuck in the air.

Clients notice the clean, clear energy as soon as they come into my space. It is my routine to clean the space every day. It takes five to ten minutes and it makes me feel great. In fact, I need this more than the clients do. Remember my altar. My work space is an altar, with everything in its place. Each item has a space and that space must be clean. Examine your space, your place. If you feel that you need a major spring-cleaning, start with that before you do anything else.

I keep my workspace simple with few distractions. I like a big, open space, about 500 to 600 square feet, though I have worked just about everywhere. I set up the room with two chairs and a massage table. I have shelves for books, sacred things, and other objects like ocean stones, incense, and sweet grass. I also establish places for such items as a stereo, the oils, the Aranizer, the gong, Buffy's bed, and the didgeridoo.

> *Robert, a thirty-one-year-old real estate developer, came to see me. We worked on some basic healing issues such as stress, relationships, and money. As we were closing he commented that he was impressed with how clean my space felt. He said he was having trouble selling a couple of houses and he asked me to come over and cleanse them. I found this to be interesting work, providing a change of scenery. I used sage, the Cleanse spray, and a few feathers to move the air. I set intention for the space to hold Light, lifting people as they entered the doorway. I playfully set energy in place by telling Robert to visualize people walking in the door and feeling at home, not wanting to leave. He sold each place right after I cleansed them. This will not become a big part of what I do, yet it is interesting how it presented itself and the validation I felt as Robert recognized my clean space.*

STONES, CRYSTALS, AND MINERALS

I am practical in my use of crystals and stones. I like crystals and use a few in my practice. I primarily use stones for grounding and absorbing negative energy.

I collect stones wherever I go, and always from the beach in Southern California. There is a particular beach where I have been instructed by the "voice" to collect round ocean stones. The "voice" says to pick up stones that are lying in pairs, to use them in my practice, to have people hold them and place them on their bodies to ground and absorb negative energies.

The first time I was sent to this beach was September 12, 2001. I woke up that morning and heard, "Go to the beach. Get in the water and wash away the fear." So I did, and when I came out of the water, I was told to start writing this book and to start collecting these ocean stones. They were lying together in pairs and were giving off energy and calling to me. The energy coming off the pairs of stones was like the heat coming off the pavement on a hot day; I saw heat waves over the stones I was to pick up, while the other stones appeared dead, without energy. I came home with a shirt and hat full of stones—mostly round sandstone ocean rock, ranging in color from white to tan to gray, about one to four inches across.

I am sent to gather stones every three to four months, usually on the solstices and equinoxes or on a full moon. These are good times to be at the beach because the energy is so strong, and I believe some of this energy is captured in the stones, increasing their power and effectiveness as healing tools.

Now I bring along a backpack and a bag and carry out as many stones as I can. The chosen stones are powerful. When a pair of stones fits a client perfectly, I give them away. This is exciting, because I can see the way I have been guided to distribute them, and I believe this is leading the work somewhere. I am not exactly sure where, but now that I am trusting God to lead me, knowing everything is not as important as it used to seem.

The use of the stones is something unique and it is a particular trademark with the healing work. I do not know of anyone else being guided to work this way. If there is, I would be comforted to know about it. A set of stones is included in the healing kits offered on my website. Refer to the Healer Training appendix for additional information.

Stones help people anchor to the earth and the ocean, and also gives people something to hold onto as their vibration rises. I tell my clients to release their fear into the stones. They tell me how they love these rocks, wanting to know where I got them, and that is usually my cue to give them the stones.

Stones are also measuring devices that allow me to check a person's energy. When I remove the stones from their hands, I feel the heat and energy that has been transferred into the stones. This is a good gauge for how much the person has opened his heart—hands are an extension of the heart. When the heart opens, the stones get very hot. People with strong healing capabilities heat the stones the most, and they also have an inherent ability to work with energy, evident in the stones. When we raise the vibration very high it gets stored in the stone and can be used to remind the body of this experience. Many people start to vibrate as soon as they hold the stones again. I have seen this happen so much that I do not question it anymore. It is God's way of providing a connection to two of his greatest creations: the ocean and the earth (stone).

Figure 6. Ocean Stones

I use other ocean stones on the body to help release negative energy. They vary in size and shape, as they tend to be more triangular and heart-shaped instead of round. I place them on the chakras, particularly the heart, solar plexus, stomach, and pelvis. I tap lightly on the stones and send sounds to them with cymbals, a didgeridoo, tuning forks, and a drum. I use them to help people feel more grounded. I also place large stones around the feet to further assist in anchoring or grounding.

Stones do not accumulate negative energy easily. When they do, I find that the energy diffuses and releases within a few minutes. Nevertheless, I like to give regular cleansings to all of my tools, including the ocean stones.

CLEANSING

I clean each stone and each tool that I use every few months. The big cleanse happens when I wash them in sea salt water and set them outside under a full moon overnight. To make this solution, I add sea salt to purified warm water. If you live by the ocean you could wash them in the ocean water. For a smaller cleanse, I spray them with Cleanse and/or clear them with sage. I cleanse crystals the same way. When I do an overall cleansing, I also cleanse the larger, twenty-five pound pieces of crystal, stone, and other items in my space, because they have a tendency to pick up old stagnant energy, and also dust and dirt. I notice the dust in the healing space has a different static vibration to it than regular dust; after all, it is residue left over from releasing toxic negative energy. Dust and static energy need to be cleansed out of your space and off of your tools regularly.

The following are examples of the other stone types and sizes that I use and the places where I obtain them. These sizes fit comfortably in a person's hands.

Figure 7. Stones from Peru, Sedona, and Santa Barbara

I use some powerful balancing stones called Boji stones. They are smaller than the typical ocean stones I use and very powerful. Bojis are used to balance energy and get it moving. According to people who mine Boji stones, the mineral is referred to in ancient alchemy as the "philosopher stone." Owners of the land where the Boji mine is located (apparently there is only one), Karen and Jerry Gillespie are the stones' guardians. Good gem stores will be able to help you get a set of Boji stones. I like these stones because they are very metallic and have a way of getting a person's energy balanced and moving quickly. In recent times I have been using the Bojis less because of the growing power and momentum of the ocean stones, but I still keep the Bojis clean and ready to be used at any moment.

Other stones illustrated are examples of how I use minerals in my work. If you are on a piece of land to which you feel connected, ask permission from the owner, or at least from the land itself, to take a rock. Use it and work with it until you understand its properties and how to apply them to your healing work.

Dave, a fifty-five-year-old movie stuntman came to see me with a worn-out, aching body. He was rather skeptical about healing work, but had been hearing about it and thought he should give it a try. I started him off holding the Bojis, and he was about to throw them out of his hands at one point. He said, "What are these things? Do they have a current or a vibrator in them?" I laughed and told him that was his energy, that these stones were just grounding the energy. He could not believe it, and commented, "These things must be kryptonite." I showed them to him afterwards and he was amazed. I told him the more we balanced his energy and got it moving, the more his body could heal and repair itself. In his case, there was permanent damage in places where we could release energy in order to bring him relief and healing. Dave has taken up yoga and is committed to rehabilitating his body.

Figure 8: Male (left) and Female (right) Boji Stones

CRYSTALS

I use crystals like a wand to conduct energy. Sometimes when the client is balanced and vibrating, which is usually toward the end of a session, I place one crystal, pictured below, in their left hand to pull creativity and feminine energy into their body. This quartz crystal belonged to my friend Tim and was given to me after he died. It was highly charged when I received it. I think it is a special crystal and it carries some of his energy. I did not use it for a long time in the work, then one day I was guided to start using it, probably by Tim. I have seen some amazing things happen as I use this crystal. Many people have wanted it or one like it. My intuition tells me it is a conductor for Tim to send healing energy to people. I cleanse and purify it when I feel it may be losing power.

MINERALS

Michael Sutton, a friend I have mentioned a few times, is an expert in the use of stones and crystals. Several years ago he shared information with me about his knowledge of many of

Figure 9. Quartz Crystal

these minerals. Two minerals he shared with me were azurite nodules. I place these little blue stones with specks of malachite on the corner of a client's eyes to help clear their vision and third eye.

> *Lane, a seventeen-year-old high school student, received some healing work from me. I could tell he was gifted psychically and in our work together I focused awareness on his abilities. I used the azurite nodules in the corners of his eyes and a piece of meteor on the third eye. His vision opened and he was seeing his aura, as well as energy around people and plants, when we were finished. The azurite and meteor helped to ground and balance his already existing gift. With these minerals we were able to fine-tune his psychic vision so that it could open in ways he could understand. Lane was very excited about his newfound discovery.*

Figure 10. Azurite Nodules, Moldavite, and a piece of Meteor

I often use pieces of meteor early in a breathing session. I place these pieces on the third eye, on the forehead between the eyebrows. A type called moldavite looks dark, almost black, but if you hold it up to the light, the color is a pale, transparent green. I use another meteor fragment, more dense and metallic than moldavite, which I also place on the third eye, causing the third eye to relax very nicely. And once the third eye is relaxed, it is easier to open one's visual ability. As the vision opens you can see into your mind's eye; the imagination becomes active and pictures start to play like a movie in your mind. It is a powerful experience, especially if it pertains to some area where you have been blind (blocked). When using azurite nodules or meteors, you should cover the stones with an eye pillow to hold them in place.

In conclusion, I use ocean stones to balance and absorb excess negative energy. As we raise the vibration of energy in the body, the stones give my client something to hold. When they are nervous or afraid, the stones help them feel more grounded. Stones also help in balancing a person's energy and can be used in a regular practice. Many people sleep with their stones. Sometimes I wonder if that's getting a little too close, but people grow very attached to their stones; anything that helps them sleep, they say. I use crystals to draw in feminine creativity, much like a magic wand. And lastly, I use other minerals to help balance and open specific energy centers or chakras. Each stone, crystal, and mineral has a purpose. The key is to combine its healing properties with what a person needs. That is the gift of the healer.

Music

I play peaceful and relaxing music during healing sessions as atmosphere and background filler. I go through phases with various artists and specific music, preferring music that is simple and usually instrumental, featuring the flute, drums, piano, or didgeridoo. One artist whose music I frequently play is R. Carlos Nakai, a Native American flute player.

In combination with music, I include other sounds and play the didgeridoo, gong, drums, rattles, and bells. These sounds complement the recorded music, creating a flow within a person's subconscious mind. Music also helps keep a person focused, undistracted by external noises.

I start the music at the beginning of the energy work, setting the rhythm for the early part of the breathing. Sometimes I drum to get a person started with the breath, which helps with the rhythm of the breath and keeps the tempo upbeat. Music moves the client through the early stages of breath work, which is the most difficult part. The brain is doing its best to stay in control, so the atmosphere created in the beginning with music, oils, stones, eye pillow, and touch is crucial to the remainder of the session. My intuition plays a role in the selection of the music with most people.

As the client starts to open, it is best to play music that has a steady rhythm. This assists in the emotional release process. As they go deeper into the process, play very gentle music, like the flute.

There is no "right" music. Experiment, and keep your ears open for music you like and music that stimulates you. Some of the albums I play include:

+ Krishna Das, *Breath of the Heart*, Karuna LLC, 2001

+ R. Carlos Nakai, any CD, Canyon Records

+ Gabriel Roth and the Mirrors, *Ritual*, Raven (Rock Bottom), 1990

+ Dean Evenson, Li Xiangting, *Tao of Healing*, Soundings of the Planet, 2000

+ Russell Paul, *The Yoga of Sound* – Shakti Yoga, Relaxation Co., 2000

+ Russell Paul, *The Yoga of Sound* – Shabda, Relaxation Co., 2000

+ Al Gromer Khan, *Tantra Drums*, New Earth Records, 1998

+ Scott Huckabay, Dean Evenson, A.B., Daniel Paul, Gina Salan, Sonic Tribe, *Soundings of the Planet*, 2000

+ Enigma, *Enigma 1*, Atlantic Records, 1991

+ Enigma, *The Cross of Changes*, Virgin Record, 1994

+ Kenny Loggins, *Return to Pooh Corner*, Sony, 1994

+ Soul Food, *Breathe*, RYKO Disc, 1998

- Enya, *Watermark*, Warner Bros., 1988

- Paul Horn, *Inside the Great Pyramid*, Kuck Kuck Records, 1977

- Paul Winter, *Whales Alive*, Living Music, 1987

HEALTH PRACTICES

Cleanses, Bodywork and Exercise

If I fail to take care of myself, who will? If you answered, "God," you would be right. Nonetheless, I do the best I can to support God and his work with me.

It is my responsibility to know what my body needs to function at its best. This includes the type of exercise, food, and supplements I require, and the amount of sleep and any bodywork necessary to feel my best. The correct balance of all of these help me to be a clear conduit, a clear channel, for the work. When I am not in tip-top shape, it affects my work, and it affects God's work. Taking care of myself grounds me in my life, my work and myself.

As I mentioned earlier in the Energy section, I recently got a little lethargic during the holiday season. I have found that now that I am well past forty, it takes more consciousness within my body to get in shape. My metabolism is slower to respond to my intentions. More sluggish, it takes extra tuning on my part and a finer sensitivity than in the past. To do this I have to get consistent exercise and eat less sugar, fat, and dead food. I shift over to as much live food as possible, such as vegetables, fruits, juices, and easily digested proteins like tempeh, tofu, beans, and spirulina. It also helps me to do a good cleanse. Two to three weeks of this kind of focus always ends my lethargic periods.

There is a lot of information available today about blood types as they relate to nutritional needs, and I suggest you get familiar with it. Each blood type is related to specific food groupings, supplements, and cleanses. I am blood type O, so I look at this information and follow what resonates with me. A good book on the subject is *Eat Right For Your Type* by Dr. Peter J. D'Adamo with Catherine Whitney, published by Putnam.

Cleanses

My body responds well to cleanses, which fine-tune my body and help me release unwanted toxins, clear my energy, and ground me. I do one of the following cleanses every fall and spring:

- The Cleanse offered by a Sikh organization can be found on the Internet at www.thecleanse.com. This is the most thorough cleanse I do and it is excellent.

- The Cleansing Trio is available from YLEO at www.youngliving.com. This cleanse focuses mainly on the colon and liver. Not just a detox, it is based on a nutritional program that strengthens the immune system as you cleanse.

- The Master Cleanse is a good general cleanse consisting of lemons, water, cayenne pepper, and maple syrup. You usually use psyllium husk with it.

- Advanced Naturals and Renew Life are companies with excellent cleanse products.

- Colonics are a great way to irrigate and clean a toxic colon. I like colonics used in conjunction with any of the aforementioned cleanses. The colonic will remove any of the toxins not being released through the colon. During a cleanse it is very important to not reabsorb the old stuff being released.

Before choosing among the various cleansing programs available, I suggest that you get medical supervision. Once you begin to search for a cleanse that resonates with you, you will generally find the support you need. Health food stores are good for obtaining information; they have books and reading material on the various cleanses.

A pastry chef, Mark, had never done a cleanse. He found out about the Master Cleanse and at first had mixed results–he was having trouble not tasting his pastries. Eventually he got into a groove with this cleanse and went for fourteen days with it. He claimed he never felt better and it was easy for him once he got past the third day. Mark lost weight and more importantly, felt great, had a return of energy, and a lightness of Spirit. He is now committed to doing a cleanse twice a year.

Bodywork

When I am overworked, bodywork is one of the fastest ways for me to recharge. It can be clearing and grounding for me to have my body worked on. Various types of bodywork are tools to use when there are lots of demands on your energy. I particularly enjoy deep tissue massage. I do not mind a little pain; it really recharges my batteries. More important than the technique, I like for my massage therapist to be very sensitive and tuned into my body. When the bodywork is very good, I usually go in very deep and almost pass out. One time in particular, I was given a massage by a very skilled therapist named Jane. While driving home, I had to stop and get something to eat—I was so open and receptive that I was drunk with energy. My vision had opened up beyond normal; I was seeing auras and halos around certain things. It was an extremely interesting experience, though I would have loved a designated driver that night. The net result was a full recharge in my body, and I felt great for several weeks. I like to get bodywork every couple of weeks.

Physical Exercise

Another way I keep myself recharged is to exercise at least every other day. It is important for me to sweat and keep my blood flowing. As I mentioned, I have blood type O, and this blood type needs to sweat and exercise vigorously and often.

I choose from a variety of exercises such as basketball, mountain bike riding, hiking, spinning, lifting weights, and yoga. These are my favorites and I rotate, trying to do each one on a regular basis as often as possible. I see people like myself who simply need exercise to feel better. Other people try to work through too much with exercise. My focus on exercise is with balance and purpose, just the right amount to help keep the mind and body strong.

CLAIRAUDIENCE/AFFIRMATIONS

Clairaudience is intuitive hearing and speaking, and is also known as the gift of prophecy. Associated with the throat charka, Clairaudience is a lesser-known gift than clairvoyance, which is a gift of sight associated with the third eye and psychics. Throughout the book I refer to the "voice;" any time I do this I am referring to the gift of Clairaudience.

In my work, I am directed by Spirit to use specific affirmations. Maybe this is not normal, yet I do not perceive it as abnormal either. Now that I have accepted my hearing as being a gift, I realize most people do not hear and perceive things the way I do. From that aspect I would say my hearing is heightened beyond "normal." I have a tendency to think of it as ordinary and have to be reminded by others that it is something they are not as skilled at. However, I have seen people involved in this work become very heightened through their throat chakras, and start to develop gifts of hearing and sound. It is very exciting to be a witness to that.

Affirmations result from the Clairaudience. In this case, it is not just about creating an assertion of truth or a positive statement. I use affirmations to take the work deeper into a person's consciousness. I may work with statements about a perceived truth, or I may work in an opposite way to get a person's energy moving.

For instance, a corporate lawyer named Cal came to me with very definite ideas about who he was and what his problems were. He was very bright but not very open, especially with his emotion; he was very guarded. His wife had persuaded him to see me. As I worked with his energy, I was guided to have him speak some affirmations. I had him say, "People tell me how open I am. I love everyone. I cannot stand judgmental people." He started to laugh, so I asked him what was going on. He said, "You are way off." I said, "Oh, really? Okay, say these: 'People tell me I am shut down. I do not love anyone. I am very judgmental. I should just be a judge.'"

His energy shifted, and he started to open up and get emotional. He said his father was shut down and died of a heart attack at age forty. He really did not want to die that way. With Cal, the affirmations worked because he was trying to figure me out, to size me up. When I easily shifted positions, he may have lost some of his lawyer assuredness. Whichever the case, his emotions and energy were ready to open and they did. It surprised him. The way I use affirmations are in a finessed way; sometimes I use them to get through fear, sometimes to move through resistance, sometimes to give someone hope. It varies and happens through what I hear. The connection to my truth gives me the confidence to approach a person very easily with the affirmations. It is a gift that has developed nicely over the years and I am aware of how much I trust it now.

An RN named Kathy came to see me. She was a sensitive woman with little self-confidence. We worked together and cleared her energy quite fast. She was open to receive and embrace change. I could tell that she was ready to leap forward in her life. As she opened her heart and was vibrating really high, I had her say, "I have a very sensitive heart. Very few people know who I really am." She started to cry. Then I had her say, "My sensitivity is a gift. I just need to learn how to trust it." She agreed, and said, "People always open up to me, they trust me." I had her say, "That is what makes me such a great nurse."

She sobbed some more. Then I explained to her about boundaries, and being able to use her sensitivity as a gift. We worked together some more and she soon decided that she was not only a nurse, but also a healer. I have watched her develop and her confidence is much stronger now. In our work together, I used affirmations to strengthen her belief in herself in a very pure way. The affirmations were what I heard her heart say. She told me she never felt so seen or heard as in our work together.

Have you ever noticed a tennis player's racket arm? The muscle is much more developed compared to the other arm. That is how I look at my Clairaudience—it is an area that I am gifted in, having spent years honing and developing it.

I hear statements that are not necessarily worded like an affirmation when I hear them. For instance with Cal, the "voice" said, "He is not open. He does not know how to love. He is very judgmental." Out of these statements I created the affirmations to work within his belief system. In this way, the affirmations went directly to his core at precisely the right moment. That is the key to Clairaudience and this work—timing. When the "voice" delivered the statements, it confirmed Cal was ready to open. I knew Spirit was on standby. It is very exciting to watch Spirit work this way.

I did not think of these statements as affirmations until my clients asked me to repeat what I had them repeat during a session. Sometimes I can barely remember what I have them affirm while I watch how their energy moves. The affirmation may be the opposite of what is true, bringing out their humor or resistance. It is about moving energy, creating the space for God to do his work. It is not about trying to appear intuitive or psychic. I just follow the "voice" that guides me, and I try to stay out of the way with my mind and ego. The "voice" has never let me down.

You can get so much from one well-placed affirmation. All the tools contribute to the effectiveness and timing of affirmations. The breath, oils, ocean stones, and music all help raise your vibration and put your energy up against or through the block. An affirmation helps guide energy, pushing it through the block or bringing awareness to an area that has just released old energy or a fearful thought. Affirmations are effective tools in healing work.

You do not have to be Clairaudient to work with affirmations; you just need the experience and confidence to trust your intuition, which comes with time and training. This can all be developed. See the Healer Training appendix for additional information.

COLLAGES

A collage is a collection of images that make up one big picture. Many of us have created collages, perhaps as children, or as class projects in high school or college. If you have never tried making a collage, you will find it to be quite enjoyable. This creative activity can work to manifest something you want into your life.

First, let me define how a collage can achieve its full potential. A collage can be a collection of images, words, symbols, or objects, or all of them together, forming one overall picture or image. Some people call them treasure maps. I like this reference, as collages bring dreams to life.

I have made them and I have seen them enough to know how well they work. When you can activate a person's imagination and get them to take action to confront their dreams, miracles can happen. As difficult as that may be, once they express dreams as images in a collage, the collage takes on a life of its own, and creates its own miracle.

I recommend a collage when a client seems to lack focus about what they want, or they have trouble imagining how to get there. If a person is ready to take action in their life, the collage may totally possess them. I find it interesting how some people choose to complete them, and whether they are excited about their work or embarrassed by the statement it reveals. Embarrassment can stifle the whole process.

Have fun with collage, and try not to see it as work. Give your dream room enough to breathe, grow, and change to fit you. There is no right or wrong way to build a collage.

COLLAGE EXERCISE

Write down the subject of your collage (i.e., love, a job, car, house, health, relationship). This will help you focus.

List the characteristics of the subject. For example, if your subject is a new job, list the ideal elements of the job you are looking for: less stress, a feeling of accomplishment, more money, opportunity for advancement, learning experience.

Briefly describe images that pop into your head when you think about the subject.

Collect or draw pictures and words that depict your subject and its characteristics. For example, for a new job you could include a picture of a successful executive, the phrases "fulfillment," "making a difference," or "destiny," or a picture of a person in the environment in which you would like to work.

Create a three-dimensional representation of your dream using a large poster board, a box, a foam shape, or a circular hoop. Play with your images and when they are as you want them, glue them in place.

Activate your subconscious. Really look at your collage, the words you have chosen, and the images. Be aware of the feelings they evoke. You are communicating with the universe, telling the universe what you want.

Place your collage where you can see it and focus on it for the next few weeks in order to manifest your dream.

Sandy came to me complaining about a lack of a love life. I suggested that she do a collage. Excited by the idea, she started right away. Her purchases included a poster board three feet by three feet, a glue stick, and several magazines. When I heard from her a few weeks later, she was bogged down with gluing images to the board because she kept changing her mind. Apparently all the images were laid out on the board, but she kept playing "jigsaw puzzle" with the placement. As we discussed this problem, it emerged that this was her pattern with men and relationships. Making up her mind and committing to something was her admitted fault. Once this was discovered, we worked on her belief system about commitment and cleared the fear she carried about being hurt.

Sandy completed her collage, which showcased many images about assuring a good relationship. There were couples in love shown holding hands, kissing, vacationing, buying a home, painting the house, getting married, having babies, and settling down. It was a very effective collage for Sandy, and within six months she met Mr. Right and they embarked successfully into a relationship.

Collage is a powerful way of setting intention. I believe it allows you to be active in sending this message to yourself and the universe. The combination of the collage and the healing work creates a powerful vortex of Spiritual momentum. Once a person claims their dreams and is clear about their intention, the universe seems to go along with the program. It definitely works when you are willing to let God interpret your images, dreams, and desires, and trust him to send you what is best.

DREAMS/ AMBITIONS/ INTENTIONS

Our human ability to realize our wildest dreams sets us apart as a species. When you are able to communicate to yourself and to others the nature of your dreams in a comprehensible way, you have an asset that will move you along on the Spiritual path. The focus of your intentions, ambitions, and dreams give you hope and keeps you motivated. While some people characterize dreams as being lofty and unattainable, I actually consider these to be not dreams, but fantasies. What I am interested in are positive, motivating dreams that play an important role in directing us to our Life's Purpose (refer to Chapter 5), and back to it when we fall off track.

There can be a power to our dreams that strongly affects us when we lose sight of our Life's Purpose. Loss of purpose causes frustration, depression, and destructive behavior. When you reconnect to your dreams, those negative expressions will be remedied. When you are positive and hopeful, your dreams suddenly come alive, you find your passion, and creation abounds. Your Life's Purpose is confronted and your dreams do come true.

Linda's job as a commodities broker was killing her Spiritually. The pressure was too much, and her body was shutting down–she developed an ovarian cyst the size of an orange, which had to be removed, and there were also lumps forming in her breasts. I told her to get out of this job. I wanted her to make this conclusion by herself, yet if I had waited, she might not have made it. She finally "got it," gave up the job and started looking at her life. Of course, money was the big issue, so I reminded her she could not spend it if she were dead. We worked deep into her energy and discovered she had always wanted to be a writer but thought she could not make a living at it. Being a writer was a very potent dream for Linda. She was encouraged to write all through school, yet her father encouraged her to get a "real job," claiming that being a writer is not a job.

Linda started her healing process by writing about her choice to leave her career. Encouraged by her husband, she submitted her writing to a leading women's health magazine and it was accepted. From there she kept writing, and set intention to start a novel. Linda has never looked or sounded better. She is living her dream and she is on purpose with her life, which she realized is contributing to the health and healing of others.

NIGHT DREAMS

Your dreams may be night dreams, and they may be dreams that are conscious intentions of goals and desires. Night dreams originate in the subconscious when you sleep. How do you interpret them? Is there an accurate way to do this?

Night dreams are so specific to the dreamer that I rarely get involved with interpretation. I may intuit some questions, although I never feel qualified to say, "Your dream means this." That is a very subjective science. Nevertheless, the interpretation of night dreams can hold fascinating insights into our conscious and subconscious minds. If you remember your dreams, they can offer some wonderful information.

The Spirit World connects to us easily during our night dreams. Your logical mind cannot stop the transmission, although it may block you from remembering your dream in the morning. I generally remember a few dreams per night. I rarely write them down; although at times in my life, I do write them down and they prove to be very helpful to my growth.

If you work at remembering your dreams, you can get good at it. Try keeping a notebook by your bed for a week. When you wake up at night or first thing in the morning, write down your dreams. If you want to ensure that you will wake up in the middle of the night, drink one to two glasses of water before bed. When you wake up to relieve yourself, write down your dreams.

I think it is better to intuit the meanings of your dreams for yourself, and if you get stuck, ask for feedback from one or two people who you feel are intuitive to draw your own conclusions. Dream interpretation is a subjective science; if you can develop your own navigation system here you will be better off.

If your dream work is fruitful, ask to be guided by your higher self. Choose an area in your life where you have confusion or blocks. Ask Spirit to work through your dreams. Relax and record your dreams, so you can map them out or remember them later on. Remember to not take yourself too seriously—let humor and harmony be a part of the process. You may find a powerful teacher rising to the surface. Let the teacher teach.

Dream interpretation may make more sense a little further down the road, perhaps six to twelve months later, as you develop this tool. At first, be open to the lessons that are obvious to you, and allow the rest to come when you are ready. Dreams are a powerful tool. I am more interested in you understanding your dreams than a Freudian or Jungian interpretation of them. Trust yourself, and trust Spirit to guide you.

FAMILY

Family plays such an important role in our overall makeup, so I have included two sections about family in this book. The primary section is in the Mirrors chapter, and it is also important to discuss family as a healing tool. I always look at my clients' family issues, whether they are aware of them or not. Most people are very aware of their family issues and start with that subject during our initial discussion. If they are unaware of their family issues, something will bubble to the surface sooner or later. Our family history holds karmic lessons for us. Family is generally one of our best teachers, if not the best one here on the earth plane.

As a healing tool, the investigation of family can be both clearing and grounding, depending on each person's needs. For instance, it would be clearing if you were able to release old family pain, and grounding if you were able to establish a more secure connection to your family. Whichever the case, family is one of the most potent mirrors for enriching your life, exploring your life, and improving your life. In traditional therapy much time is spent reviewing childhood and family issues. It is valuable work when the relationships are understood and the resid ual pain or stuck energy is cleared. I believe it is very worthwhile work when energies can be cleared in therapy. When the issues are just dealt with intellectually, then it is only partial healing. Completing the healing by clearing the energy out of the person's body and bringing the understanding of that completion to them is what we seek.

A thirty-eight-year-old, professional, single woman who had never been married, Alice said she had trouble trusting men, originating from her experiences with an alcoholic father. A proclaimed bisexual, Alice did not see much of a future with men, and her recent experiences revealed less and less optimism about relationships with women, too. In our work together we focused on her inability to trust anyone, including herself. As we worked with her energy, much anger and rage came up about men, abuse, past lives, death, and the Salem witch trials.

The mention of the name "Salem" gave her goose bumps. She always sensed that she was hung and/or burned at the stake in past lives. So we cleared some powerful energies that showed up as trauma to her neck area. Her throat was red hot and quivered much of the time. In her everyday life, she suffered from throat issues such as a sore throat, squeaky voice, trouble breathing, and hesitancy to speak up to authority figures, especially those that were male. It was interesting work, and we followed it through. There were mini-exorcisms as these fear-based dark energies were cleared away.

Eventually Alice opened to a relationship with Brian, a good man whom she grew to love and trust. When she took Brian to meet her dad, they got along great. Alice was quite relieved that her father did not embarrass her. A couple of years later they married. I pointed out to her that as she healed, she was able to open herself to love from a man. This love allowed her to return to her father and heal her relationship with him— Alice grew to accept her father because Brian accepted him so easily. She has come a long way in a few years time, and now she has a baby boy. Spirit never ceases to amaze me, and I love seeing families come back together and complete circles of healing.

There are many psychological issues in this situation, and lots of conclusions that can be drawn. What is important to me is that Alice healed her life. She healed her relationship with men and with the masculine energy by which she felt abused. Ultimately her mom and dad, who had been estranged, were able to come back together as friends, especially in celebration of the grandbaby.

PRAYER

I grew up thinking that prayer was a burden. Raised Catholic, I still have the prayer book I was given for my First

Communion. Praying the way I saw it practiced in church seemed antiquated to me, even as a child; since then, prayer has evolved into a conversation I have with God. I speak from my heart in my own words. My intent behind prayer is what is most important, not the arrangement of the words or the rhythm in which they are said. Many ancient teachings disagree with this and I acknowledge the basis and power of these teachings; however, I am looking at the entrance point for many people, and that is simplicity. Once they harness the simplicity of prayer, they can move on to explore other ways of prayer.

I believe the essence of God lies in our hearts, especially when we choose to love. Prayer spoken from the heart finds universal ears and pathways to other hearts. Praying from the head or in an idealistic way does not resonate with me. I do not care about what someone knows in his or her head; I do care what he or she feels within the heart. This kind of prayer works for me. If doing Buddhist chants, the rosary, or reading from the Bible, Koran, Kabbalah, or Bhagavad Gita works for you, then do that. There is no right way to pray, there is only what works for you.

I relate to prayer as a tool. It can be clearing if it helps you release, and grounding if it helps you connect to God.

FULL MOON

The full moon is a powerful healing tool. I use it to cleanse the physical tools that I use in the work. There is something about cleansing my tools and setting them outside under the full moon to recharge. This cleansing under the moon seems to freshen up the energy contained in each tool or sacred object.

The full moon is also a strong stimulator of issues, because the moon pulls on the tides of one's emotions just like it pulls on the tides of the ocean. The emotions reside in the second chakra, the water area of the body. When your emotions are pulled, you may get tense and frustrated. Add sexual tension, which also gets stimulated by the moon, and you end up with a lot of energy that needs to move. Refer to the Chakra and Sexuality chapters for additional information. The full moon always proves to be a powerful healing time, for both clients and healers.

In the healing work, I am always aware of the full moon. Although other phases of the moon are important too, such as the new moon, I find the full moon is the most powerful phase.

> *Without fail, my phone gets much busier five to six days before and up to the full moon. Recently Karen, a real estate agent, called me up hysterically. She thought she was losing her mind, had been missing work, and did not want to leave her home. I told her she was feeling the affects of the moon, which was about to be full in a couple of nights; I told her to hang in there. She acquiesced slowly, saying she forgot about the moon, but she was very aware of her PMS. I reminded her that she was very emotional on the last full moon. She finally agreed, and a couple days later she called and confirmed that she felt fine. Usually after the moon peaks the energy starts to relax and people lighten up dramatically. Full moons hold more intensity for Karen because her periods fall during this time, too. I am always amazed how Karen and many other people forget about the effects of the moon from month to month.*

I also notice the tension on the roads as drivers are more aggressive during this time. Police departments report increased violence and crime rates, and there is increased activity in emergency rooms. It is a real phenomenon and it pays to be aware of the moon's pulls on our emotions and energy.

Within this awareness, there are many benefits to the moon's energy. Full moon is a time of increased light in the night sky, an opportunity to see and feel in the dark. The moon cycle has correlations to women's cycles and rhythms of fertility and germination in nature. I recognize an increased connection to my instinctive feminine side, which is validated if I get out in nature at night and during the daylight hours on the days of full moon. Everything is heightened. It is especially important for me to get to the ocean during this time, too. This is a natural phenomenon that we are fortunate to have here on earth—it opens our imagination to the connection of the earth, sun, and moon. I relish the time with the full moon.

OTHER HEALING TOOLS

Other tools that play a role in my work are the gong, sweet grass, juniper, the didgeridoo, an eye pillow, pau santo wood, incense, Native American shields, and rose quartz.

Gong

I use a large gong made by the Paiste Gong Company. The vibrations it produces are particularly clearing, helping to move the client to a deeper state of consciousness, and allowing the work to go deeper. The gong creates a strong healing vibration and sound.

> *Randy, a young musician, heard the gong and immediately opened to a deep kundalini (refer to Chapter 6) awakening as I played it. He said he had never before felt vibrations move like this through his body. It took me several minutes to bring him back as our session ended. As a musician he was open to sound and vibration and it took him for a very deep ride.*

Sweet Grass

Often used in Native American sweat lodges, this braided, long grass stem works somewhat like sage. It is very clearing and has a sweet smell.

> *Allison, twenty-two, was new to Spiritual work. When she smelt sweet grass, it created a sense memory for her and it took her back to a lifetime as a Native American. She was in it so deeply she started speaking the Native language for several minutes. She remembered many experiences during this lifetime.*

Sweet grass can have a very deep hypnotic effect on some people. It is always gentle and peaceful though, and I trust this plant to guide people much as I do with sage.

Juniper/Cedar

Juniper is an evergreen tree in the cedar family. Its clearing properties are very strong and I use it most often in ceremony for a deep cleanse before an initiation. As a clearing plant, juniper compliments sage very nicely. Years ago, I was participating in an initiation with my friend Tim. I thought he used juniper because it was handy and I tended to overlook its clearing properties at the time, yet I always remembered the smell of this evergreen tree and the power it had to clear old energy. I use it more now and I have some special trees in Arizona and New Mexico that drop me little bundles in the night. I think this is a natural response for the tree during dry weather and I just pick its offerings off the ground.

Didgeridoo

This is an aboriginal native musical instrument from Australia. Made from a hollowed out tree trunk, it is one of the oldest instruments known to man. Blowing into the didgeridoo creates vibrations and healing sounds that can be directed into areas of the body where energy is stuck, helping it move. It is also a powerful tool for clearing.

> Paul, at age fifty-seven, came to me with many alternative views and modalities under his belt as a chiropractor. When I used a didgeridoo over his body, he began shaking all over. He said he could feel the vibration into his core and throughout his nervous system. He claimed he had never felt his heart open so wide as when I blew the didgeridoo into it. Paul responded much like Randy did with the gong.

These incidents show me that as a person opens up, they are very responsive to further opening with timely and precise sound vibrations. Once we get a person into the furthest reaches of consciousness through healing, it leaves a lasting impression on them about who they really are. In this expanded state, visions and awakenings occur. Many people tell me they have never experienced anything like this work. Tools like the didgeridoo can be icing on the cake in a healing session.

Eye Pillow

Covering your client's eyes helps to relax the brain and allows him or her to drop into a meditative state without distractions. I also use an eye pillow to hold stones and meteorites in place on the third eye. Someone once commented that my eye pillows must contain a lot of tears. I agreed and said that was why I had three, so I could rotate them. (I also wash, cleanse, and clear them from time to time.)

Pau Santo Wood

From South America, this is an ancient wood with tremendous clearing properties when burned. The first time I smelled it, the odor took me home to a familiar place—it has a smell like some ancient incense. Originally, a piece of this wood was given to me by a man named Mauro in Cusco, Peru. He heard I was a healer and took me to a market for shamans. He burned the wood for me and showed me how to use it. I was able to get a small bundle of it to bring home with me.

I burn pau santo during my workshops, and it helps to deepen the work by stimulating old memories and deeper connections with our souls. One of my clients, Daniel, smelled pau santo during his session and said to me, "What is that smell? It's taking me back to an ancient time. Where can I get some of that?" The power of the wood lies in the experience it creates. I compare it to the power of sage and/or frankincense.

Incense

To use incense in healing work, I light it for a few seconds to add its particular energy to the room. I use it sparingly. My favorite incenses are made by Fred Soll; they include Frankincense Champa, Dragon's Blood, Magical Copal, Desert Patchouli, Ceremonial Rain, Lovely Lavender, Taos Pine, and other aromas. I do not like to be overwhelmed by a perfume-scented incense. Unlike synthetic smells or vibrations, these all smell like plants, which seems to be better in this work. I like the subtleties and the hint of an essence to stimulate memories. Incense can definitely help in that process.

Native American Shields

These shields are displays of my collected medicine, placed in the healing room for protection from negative forces. These forces could include dark energies or entities not wanting to be identified or released in a person, and can be very subtle. I find the shield grounds me as I work and helps keep me clear from distractions. A shield may consist of animal skins, feathers, symbols, and other healing tools and objects. (I discussed Shields earlier in Native American Medicine.)

Rose Quartz

I have a large piece of rose quartz in my healing room to help me stay clear as I work. I feel its particular vibration in the room. This particular piece of rose quartz weighs about twenty-five pounds and is quite substantial. A mineral this large has a tendency to collect energy over time, so I clean it once every two to three months.

Tool Cleansing Techniques

These techniques include washing objects, such as rocks and crystals, in sea salt water; spraying things, such as cloths, feathers, and the room, with Cleanse spray; and smudging objects, like animal skins, medicine shields, or the room, with sage. Finally, place whatever you can outside under a full moon (refer to Full Moon section).

In addition to the tools mentioned in this chapter, collect your own. Find objects that resonate with you. There are no rules or absolutes about healing tools. They are simply objects used to facilitate healing work, and are not the work itself. Oils, sage, and the other tools I mentioned are not mandatory to do the work, but they can certainly help.

Figure 11. Native American Shield

CHAPTER FIVE

LIFE'S SPIRITUAL PURPOSE

In this new millennium, we are hip to change. We know there must be more out there than we are now experiencing, and much of this readiness to change is due to the age of instant information and reality-based awareness on television and the Internet. People come to me with many tools, seminars, therapy, and training under their belt, yet they cannot seem to put it all together. Of course, manifestation is what they focus on, not the process—we are a results-oriented society.

To help my clients develop their clarity, I ask them to back up and look at the process, or the journey, rather than the desired result. In our early work together, we explore their life's Spiritual purpose; from there, we see how dreams and interests feed off that purpose. Then we set realistic goals or time lines, and we create affirmations to energize the goals and create a positive atmosphere. I often recommend an art project, such as a collage, to activate the subconscious and generate ideas. The next step is fulfillment: taking actions to bring life to the graphic elements and the concepts in the collages.

Leslie, a thirty-eight-year-old advertising executive, came to me with lots of misery and very little hope for a relationship.

She said she worked so much she had no time for a life. She liked making money, yet was now realizing her lifestyle did not afford her happiness. I suggested a collage.

She created an advertisement of the life she wanted, an incredibly fancy and creative collage of wonderful images of the relationship of her dreams. Intimacy was a hot topic in this layout. Vacations, children, and a dog were all included. She was active with tennis, hiking, and yoga, and her body was sculpted and in shape. There was an amazing depiction of her home, and she conveyed her comfort level in this place with relaxed, lived-in photos. All of this was connected to her occupation in the advertising world; however, her relationship to her work was specifically changed. Leslie created a company logo with her name on it, as the owner, instead of working for someone else, and it was clearly communicated that she had abundant support and staff with this new company. Balance was conveyed and the work portion of the collage did not outweigh any other area. The collage came across as her personal photo album: she placed herself in an array of the pictures so that you believed this was her real life now. Leslie's collage proved to be very effective in its magnetism and I have seen her create or move towards everything that showed up in the collage advertisement of her life.

With a completed collage, we demonstrate a faith that the work is done and we release our expectation for an outcome. This allows for universal synchronicity or magic to happen, which gets the goose bumps started as Spirit comes closer to manifesting what we want.

For you to better understand the process of discovering your life's Spiritual purpose, I will break down each step. We all have a Spiritual purpose in life. Some spend their lives avoiding their purpose because it seems overwhelming or unrealistic. Do you know this feeling? Can you understand that this is where rebellion comes from?

My biggest obstacle in training people to do healing work is the belief that they could not help someone else when they do not feel healed themselves. Deep down they know they have healing ability, yet there is an overwhelming reluctance to trust it. It is a push-pull feeling. Nevertheless, something (Spirit) brought them to me. Many have said they know they are healers, and as we start to confront that, a fear creeps in and for some, a rebellion may occur. Of course, Mr. Reluctance (me) recognizes all of the resistance that appears around life's Spiritual purpose as a healer. Fear makes dreams seem unrealistic; the feeling can be overwhelming, thus creating rebellion or resistance to move ahead.

Earlier, I mentioned the call for the awakening of your soul, and this is what I am talking about here. When you are on purpose in your life, the call for the awakening of the soul can occur. Yes, it is Spiritual, and it is also practical. For instance, when you do what you love to do—and you love it enough that you would to do it for free—you will receive financial rewards and a flood of good energy.

When I am involved in my purpose, such as writing this book, I feel energized, excited, hopeful, positive, and passionate. As I worked through fear and doubt, I felt clearer and clearer about the information. It is amazing how fear and doubt distracted me from my purpose in the past.

I help people discover their life's purpose with my healing and healer training work. I look at this work as all encompassing, whether someone is receiving a healing session, going on a healing retreat, or participating in the healer training. Once we have cleared away their illusions and deeply connected them to their truth, their purpose is apparent. The truth of who they are and what they are about is right there.

This is how I help people discover their purpose:

+ Get the person out of his or her head and into his or her heart.

- Raise the client's vibration to a high level with the breath.

- Access the client's inner child through the heart open-ing–this is the innocent, playful part of us that speaks the truth.

- Play with the inner child; connect him or her to the client's life and discuss what he or she really wants to do, and what he or she is on the earth to accomplish.

This approach works time and again. I have watched my clients change their lives in a day—a very exciting transformation to watch.

Unemployed and with a Ph.D. in paleontology, Judy came to me after some serious health issues, including a battle with cancer, caused her to reassess what she thought she wanted to do with her life. Uncertain about continuing in paleontology, she did enjoy writing her doctorate and the presentation and discussion of her project.

As I worked with her, I saw that a tremendous force moved through her; Spirit had rarely moved so strongly in a person. And, I saw that her health issues were indeed complete—she was healthy.

The "voice" told me that Judy had a tremendous gift for writ-ing. I could see that her throat chakra was red hot and very open, and was guided to let her proclaim she was a writer. As her breathing and energy started to calm down, I guided her to the little girl inside her heart. We talked with this little girl, five-year-old Judy who loved to play, have fun, and write, directly through the adult Judy. I asked more about the writ-ing and she said she was here to write, and that she would come through Judy and they would create a set of short stories about their life. It seemed like there were two distinct entities within the same body. Little Judy had a great connection to the past, and a connection equally as strong to the present.

She proclaimed she was the one with the creativity and the humor. I watched adult Judy embrace this little girl and become a writer that moment. She is currently a full-time writer.

Dreams, affirmations, collages, goals, faith/release, and magic/universal synchronicity; all of these are tools of manifestation. Dreams, affirmations, and collages are discussed in detail in the tools section—refer to them if you need to refresh your memory.

Goals are realistic projections of attainment of your dreams or desires. Timelines or dates of accomplishment are important to establish, in order to reach goals. Faith/release is "giving it up to God." After you have done the work, let go of the focus on the outcome. This is a test of faith, and either you have it or you don't. Magic/universal synchronicity is when the work is done, the outcome is released, and faith manifested. The universe conspires to reward you with synchronicity around your desires.

We all like to manifest. I am speaking beyond the physical, material worlds. Manifestation in line with your life's Spiritual purpose rewards you with great joy, celebration, and fulfillment, making a complete connection to the depths of who and what you are.

In this chapter I string things together to clarify for you how the "work" works. To be successful in life, you must be specific and plan accordingly. Luck will only take you so far. Use all of your tools and come to understand yourself better than anyone else you know. Lead the way for people to understand you by being clear about yourself. Know thyself. When you have done your work and removed what is counterproductive, then you will succeed and God will have a clear path to work through you.

Faith comes from a support system of prior action and results, and it can be a recognition that the moment of change is upon you and you have the fortitude to take the leap. I believe in "20/20 vision" faith, rather than in blind faith. If you do the work, faith will not only follow, but it will lead you and be rock solid. Whatever it takes, make contact and deliver on your life's Purpose.

Alice and Ted, both in their forties, had been married for ten years. They were healers specializing in bodywork, and both had developed their craft and trained to do healing work. I witnessed much growth within the time I knew them. We worked on and talked a lot about manifestation of their life's Spiritual purpose. As individuals, and as a couple, they knew their Spiritual purpose in this lifetime was to have their own healing retreat center where they worked with individuals and groups. Their dream was to purchase land and start the process soon. Their goal was to buy the land in 2002, which they accomplished. Their affirmation was: "The Center of Inner Light Healing is hosting its first healing retreat by June 1, 2003."

Ted had a background in architecture and they created a three-dimensional model of the center that revealed plans for their entire ten-acre property; it was a very effective collage. Their fulfillment actions began as they broke ground for the construction of the main lodge. Within their overall plan they had a timetable of two phases: Phase One was to get the property under way as a center with one main structure in which to live and do the work; Phase Two included more structures and development of the grounds. They knew they had enough money to complete Phase One. As is true with most construction projects, they were concerned about having funds for Phase Two. Based on the success of past workshops, they knew they could create funds doing more of these after Phase One was complete. They leaped forward with their faith and began construction of the facility. Their project was blessed with much magic and synchronicity, as they finished ahead of schedule and under-budget. And they were able to schedule a retreat on May 1, 2003, earlier than the projected June 1, 2003 opening; their manifestation was flowing beyond expectations with the The Center of Inner Light Healing.

MANIFESTATION EXERCISE

Use the formula in Figure 12 to create something you want to manifest, as per the following example.

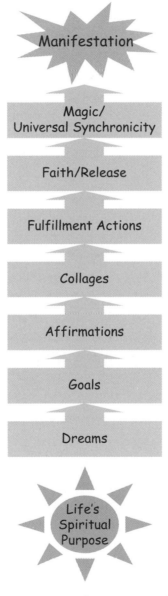

Figure 12. Manifestation Formula

Do note that the following story is an example of my original manifestation process; several things happened differently than I intended in August 2003. That is part of the beauty of this process, as the specifics of our intention gets the energy moving and we let God interpret what is best for us. Once the energy is moving, it always proves to be an enlightening experience. Thus, here is my original concept of getting the book published:

It was part of my life's Spiritual purpose to write this book. The dream, once I started the book, was to express my creativity freely, and to share my insights and knowledge. My goal was to finish the book and send it to a publisher by October 1, 2003. My affirmation was "to experience joy as my book is being published." I did a collage around the contract, visualizing the contract being signed and a picture of the finished book; I also imagined doing a book tour with signings. As fulfillment action, I contacted five publishers for whom I had leads and submitted what they requested. Faith and release was to do all the tasks I knew were necessary, then leave the outcome up to God. Magic/universal synchronicity was when a new client came in for a healing treatment not knowing that I had written the book, and he took home a copy to his wife, a publisher. Manifestation was a stack of the finished, published books sitting on my desk, seeing my book in a bookstore, and doing a book signing at a local bookstore. To repeat, this was my intention in August 2003.

Among the later developments, when I finished the book and was ready to contact the publishers, the "voice" said, "You are going to self-publish." I said, "I don't want to do that! I am ready to hand this book off to someone else." My ego wanted a good publisher, and I knew nothing of self-publishing. The "voice" said, "You are going to publish many books; you need to learn the process." I resisted, and sent in five submissions anyway, and quickly heard back from three, who rejected the manuscript.

I was directed to Simon Warwick-Smith to help guide me through the self-publishing process, and I have since adjusted several manifestation points, yet the end result is the same. I have a stack of published books on my desk, I see them in local bookstores, and I do author events.

Figure 13 depicts my seven life purpose points, which are the roles I play in fulfilling my Spiritual purpose. Currently, these points include writer, healer, father, husband, athlete, farmer, and actor. The various roles flow in and out of being the center focus point. Writer is currently at the center point.

Figure 13. Life Purpose Points

LIFE PURPOSE EXERCISE

You play more than one role in your life. Each role should be part of your life's Spiritual purpose. Examine each role you play and observe how each element of your character, each manifestation of your purpose flows in and out of the center point.

⤳

CHAPTER SIX

EASTERN INFLUENCES

Your desire to tune into the subtle aspects of your being may draw you to the concepts and teachings of Eastern philosophies. The language and terms are unique in these philosophies; if you must find your own language for these things, I believe it is okay. For instance if you do not like the word yoga, then call it stretching, exercise, or meditation. Ultimately, it comes down to what works for you and what you can relate to.

We will discuss the terms chakra and kundalini—do not let them scare you. Think of them as descriptions of energy. I keep it simple so all of us get what we need to evolve, to open, to get clear, and feel empowered. My goal is to create a universal understanding of energy and healing so this can happen.

CHAKRAS

The word "chakra" is from the ancient Sanskrit language of India, meaning "wheel" or "energy center." There is debate over the number of chakras in and around the body and their exact placement, and there is varied information about their roles and purposes in the body. People have diverse ways of sensing the chakras and using them for healing.

Again, where awareness goes, energy flows. The more aware-ness you bring to the energetic body, the more you can work through and clear the physical and energetic blocks in the body. The chakras are engines for the energetic body. As you learn to tune into each chakra, you will have more control with the direc-tion and flow of energy. Being able to use your awareness to tune into your body through the chakra system gives you a unique ability to heal yourself. Most people do not know how, nor do they trust themselves enough to tune in. That is what I am teach-ing you to do with this work.

I recognize seven major chakras in the human body. They start at the base of the spine in the coccyx area, running up the body to the top of the head. I have been able to run my hand in front of a person's body and feel the chakras. It feels like a fan blowing air into the palm of the hand. The spinning of the ener-gy tickles the hand. It is a real sensation. In some cases, I start the chakras spinning so that the person can feel them for the first time. I start the chakras spinning by passing my hand in front of the charka, finding the right distance for activation, usu-ally six to eight inches. The chakras start to spin when they are addressed with the right sensitive connection. When this hap-pens, it leaves a lasting impression because there is great intima-cy exchanged from the higher essence of each person involved. It is a soul connection facilitated by energy through the chakras. It is an exchange of love, nothing more, nothing less.

> *Many years ago, an artist named LuAnn came to me want-ing to go deeper in her Spiritual work. I recognized an open-ness and desire for growth and sensed a tremendous sensitiv-ity and connection to energy and Spirit. LuAnn was unsure of how to connect to her energy, even though she knew when she could feel it. She was at the mercy of what her energy wanted to do, not believing she could control it. I told her I would show her how.*
>
> *I ran my hand about six inches in front of her body, from crown to base. I did not expect the alignment and connection*

of energy to be so strong. As I moved my hand, I could feel her chakras activate and start to spin. I could also feel the transition from one chakra to the next and the differences between each one. Spirit gave me a glimpse of how powerful it was to connect this way. In that moment we became universal with each other; it transcended the physical and we became one. Not sexually or emotionally, but Spiritually; we were connected by Spirit. I was intrigued by this experience and have rarely felt it so detailed and strong. Ten years later, LuAnn commented that this experience opened her heart and committed her to a lifetime of Spiritual pursuits. I believe that God gave me a glimpse into the possibilities of what can be experienced in this work. Of course that carrot is dangling out there in front of me. I have learned there are many extenuating circumstances that affect this alignment—I will talk about these later in this chapter.

The location of each chakra corresponds to the location of a ductless gland. An example of a ductless gland would be the thyroid gland in the throat. These glands manufacture hormones and/or endorphins that give the body a jolt of energy, an adrenaline rush that may feel electrical or buzzy. I find that when this energy moves, it makes room for Spirit to travel through the body by opening the body's pathways.

These centers are usually activated through our "fight or flight" mechanism, rather than in a meditative way. For example, when a car falls on a child, the mother runs over and lifts the car to save the child; released through the ductless glands in the chakra system, tremendous energy shoots through the woman to save her child. You can stimulate these energy centers with the breath, which activates them in a peaceful and intentional way, enabling you to make contact with that energy source and training the body to let go of stored fears and traumas. See The Breath section for additional information.

When a person gets out of balance, one or more chakra areas may seem stuck. Fatigue and frustration will pour out of that

7 - Crown

6 - Third Eye

5 - Throat

4 - Heart

**3 - Solar
Plexus**

2 - Pelvis

1 - Base

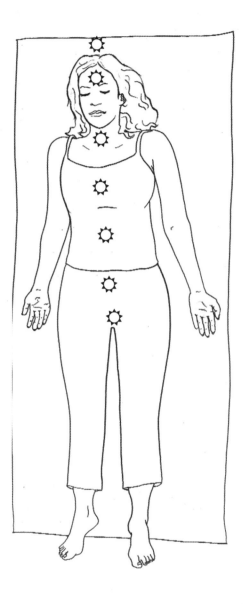

Figure 14. Chakra Front View

person. Intuitively they know something is wrong. The key is to get the Body, Mind, and Spirit back in balance.

For example, imagine a washing machine that is out of balance and trying to spin a load of laundry. It is clunking, banging, and cannot get going. You have to take out some wet, stuck-together laundry to get the washer going and to rebalance it. This is how the chakras are when they get stuck or out of balance with blocks such as stuck negative emotions: fear, anger, sadness, judgments, and stagnant energy. You have to focus on them, see what is causing the disharmony, and either take it out or rebalance it. If something is causing you to feel negative, frustrated, angry, depressed, sick, or tired, then it is time for some healing. When you are in balance you feel happy, hopeful, and full of peace. You have a stream of vitality and things seem to flow. This flowing feeling is your energy moving through the chakras. And this openness connects you to everything. It facilitates a sense of well-being, belonging, and oneness.

Working with the chakras in myself and within others is a powerful experience; when this happens, the word "connection" takes on a whole new meaning. When the chakras align and start spinning, there is an incredibly open feeling between the parties involved. I have experienced the feeling alone, but I find it most often happens with another person, an animal (Buffy), Spirit being (Ezekiel), or an entity in nature (sage or red-tailed hawks). I also felt this when my daughter was born. The spinning feeling usually starts in the sacrum area and goes right up the body, like a jet engine taking off—it feels like flying! The energy around the emotions moves right up through the heart, the throat, and out of the eyes and top of the head. It is something truly powerful, and Spirit never lets you forget the feeling.

I have also experienced this while acting. I think that is why I loved acting so much—because it was when the most magic happened for me, when time stood still and the chakras would spin and open. I experienced so much freedom in these moments.

The first time I felt this while acting I was in my first close-up on a movie set. I was nervous, not even sure I could remember my lines. The camera zoomed in close to my face as I looked into the eyes of the actress opposite me. A deep Spiritual connection occurred as our characters fell in love. I felt this spinning sensation deep in my body, and it continued spinning up my body. When it got to my throat area I could not speak for a second as I was hit with a wave of energy and emotion. The intense feelings and energy continued until we finished the scene a few moments later. When the director yelled, "Cut!" you could hear a pin drop. Magic occurred in that first close-up and from that moment on I understood why actors love their job so much.

If I could have controlled this feeling, or opened this way more predictably, I would likely have done more acting. However, God's plan for me has been more about this book, the healing work, and fatherhood. If I am meant to get back in front of a camera it will happen when the time is right. Plus, writing is proving to be very satisfying for my creativity right now.

The experience of spinning and openness which I just explained to you is what I see clients experience when I balance their chakras with my hands. This is powerful and does not always happen. I find that these openings are best facilitated in the presence of a huge amount of love, trust, and positive energy. I break it down this way:

- A person must be ready to risk change.

- A high level of energy is involved, which appears as excitement or nervousness.

- If love is backing the high-energy state, the heart opens; if fear is present, the heart will not open and the head stays in control.

- If the heart opens, love flows through and activates the charkas—this is a beautiful thing.

It is easiest to align and balance the chakras when synchronicity happens; one person opens and the other is receptive, like falling in love. So much within the human system is determined by love, one of the key facilitators of life, and perhaps that is why people are so in love with the idea of being in love. That may explain why falling in love is so intoxicating. If we could just teach people how to do this and retain their own identities, and to keep clear boundaries, it would be an even more powerful experience. When we open our chakras it is easy to open our hearts; we invite in more opportunities to experience love and life.

What are the keys to opening your heart? Can you do it yourself? When you do this for yourself, will it be easier for you to recognize when you are ready to receive love? I answer these questions in the Blocks section.

I believe the chakra system holds the key to our energy, but it's okay if we can get our energy flowing without focusing on them. I believe the chakras are tools for understanding ourselves, and if you can use the information about the chakras to understand yourself, then it is a worthwhile tool and should be used.

CHAKRA BLOCKS

Blocks are anything that stops or impedes the flow of energy and awareness. Blocks limit the ability to open and access Spirit. We strive to be open and to have magic in our lives, yet things get in the way and block this flow. The names for some of these things are negativity, wounds, anger, fear, depression, cancer, illness, sadness, abuse, tightness, sickness, stress, worry, need for control, and disease. Blocks keep us stuck and limit our growth. They are barriers to our evolution and ability to unfold. The following lists identify blocks that are common to each chakra.

Blocks to the Base Chakra

• Physical and sexual abuse

- Inability to ground or connect to earth; numbness or very little energy flowing to the feet affects a person's ability to ground himself

- Rigidity, stiffness, and contradiction, limiting a person's flexibility both physically and psychically

- Pain, especially inflammation of tailbone

An important and overlooked chakra, the base is our foundation, our grounding connection to the earth, and is often illustrated as flowing down to the earth. If a person cannot ground, they will have trouble as they walk through life. When abuse blocks the flow of energy through this area, it is easy to spot. Many times the hips and pelvis are turned inward in an attempt to conceal or protect the area. Also, a lot of weight (insulation) may be present around this area, and in some cases it literally hangs over the first chakra. When someone falls on his or her tailbone, the base is trying to get jarred free; it is not easy to explain this to someone who is in pain.

When the base areas are blocked, they are extremely sensitive to pressure or touch. The person may have severe pain or the area may be masked over with a ticklish feeling. Whichever the case, these sensations make it hard for a person to be open in their base chakra.

Unblocking the Base Chakra

- Healing work

- Yoga for flexibility

- Sweat lodges, to ground the tailbone into the earth

- Sit down next to a big tree, lean against it, hug it if necessary

- Massage

- Dance

- Anything that brings awareness to the first chakra

At age fifty-one, Lucille was a social worker who suffered from obvious blocks to her first chakra. Extremely overweight with chronic foot and leg pain, she was not grounded and had fallen several times, injuring her ankles and tailbone region. We worked with her energy and cleared a lot of anger out of her first chakra. Pain was the main connection and association to her body. Eventually she revealed she had been repeatedly abused and beaten by her parents well into her teens. There were wounds held in several of her chakras. One wound was being beaten with a wooden paddle on her bottom, and Lucille was very reluctant to look at this at first. She said she had moved on and felt nothing towards her parents now; they were both dead.

I agreed we would bring up her parents only as needed, as long as we cleared the residual anger out of her first chakra. She reiterated that she had dealt with this in therapy, and I told her it was not entirely cleared. Once she agreed, we were able to clear much of the toxic anger out of this chakra right away. There was so much rage in her body, I was amazed she was still on her feet. She had many issues about being touched, so I encouraged her to get some massages, which helped clear more energy. Then she did a sweat lodge to connect with the earth and to release stuck energy into the earth. She started taking yoga classes, which created more flexibility and integration with her body.

Lucille now feels like a different person, and she feels her ability to do her job as a social worker is greatly improved because she feels grounded and in her body. Her body is coming back to life, becoming free of chronic pain and turmoil. I noticed she has lost quite a bit of weight, although we do not focus on her losing weight. The weight melts off as her self-esteem grows.

Blocks to the Second Chakra

- Sexual abuse

- Physical abuse

- Constipation, more common with women

- Numbness, inability to physically feel in this area

- Emotions that are stuck and will not move or change

- Sugar cravings; when energy is suppressed or pushed into the second chakra, sugar is craved for satisfaction

- Eating disorders such as bulimia and anorexia

- Creativity blocks, high levels of frustration

- Shame and guilt around sexuality: blockages that stick around the ovaries and hips

- Lower back pain, which is manifested by fear and blockages regarding support and money

- Father issues, usually in the lower back

Holding the key to mastery of ourselves, the second chakra is the nuclear reactor of the chakra system, the area where most of our human earthly problems lie. Most people live from this chakra, because their life experiences are in the area of sex, food, and money. If you are locked in the second chakra you may never experience openness in the heart or clear thinking, or vision in the third eye or crown.

For example, the ovaries and the pelvic and navel areas are storehouses for creativity in a woman's body, and that creativity connects to the throat area where the energy either gets expressed or not. If there are blocks in either chakra, a woman will likely experience feelings of anger, suppression, and frustration because she cannot release or express this energy. This happens a lot with PMS and menopause. Even though these problems are generally blamed on hormone imbalances, I find the cause is blocked energy. Some women have it and some do not. There can be many reasons for hormone imbalance, and blocked energy is the main one.

Much of our global consciousness is stuck in the second chakra of the earth's population, an area that hosts much drama and chaos on the physical plane. This chakra is often so out of balance that people live their lives stuck, trying to deal with their emotions, sexual issues, creativity, food, and money. The second chakra is an area for much activity in the human body—openings, connections, and being stuck. I talk about this extensively in the Sexuality and the Second Chakra chapter.

Because it is the nuclear reactor, this chakra holds the most potential for the greatest abuse. If people are living here, how do you get them out? How do you transcend the second chakra? How do you teach your clients how to safely navigate out of this abyss without stimulation of all the gory stuff in there?

Unblocking the Second Chakra

- Healing work

- Massage

- Colonics

- Cleanses

- Yoga

- Exercise

- Release of energy and emotions

- Dance

- Anything that brings awareness to the second chakra

- See the Second Chakra Clearing Formula section for additional information

A forty-year-old librarian named Carolyn came to me complaining about being blocked in her colon. She had chronic constipation, stifling PMS cramps, annoying hot flashes, and constant lower back pain. She mentioned a history of sexual abuse by a family friend that lasted from age six to twelve. She had been working on this for years in therapy, yet the memories were still very painful. Constipation had never been connected to the abuse. Carolyn needed caffeine from coffee and sodas to have a bowel movement, and sometimes waiting over a week for the next one.

The sexual abuse caused her physical, emotional, mental, and Spiritual discord. She had confusing memories of actually enjoying the attention, thinking it must be acceptable, and that it must be love. This manipulation twisted her intestines, causing an out-of-body feeling, numbness, and disconnection. We brought awareness to her body and started clearing the energy. I worked on her belly to release old stagnant energy. She had never successfully cleared the guilt and shame that was holding the sexual abuse energy. I encouraged her to embrace her stifling PMS and not to deny it, and to use the bleeding as an energy cleanse for all the guilt and shame around the abuse. The healing has worked nicely for Carolyn: she feels completely different in her body and she is much more regular these days. PMS is not nearly as severe, the menopause condition has lightened considerably, and her lower back pain has gone away.

Blocks to the Third Chakra

- Battles of will with others

- Willfulness toward yourself

- Inability to feel second chakra emotions, inability to love with fourth chakra (Heart Center)

- Heavy reliance on masculine energy

You may think this is a male-dominated problem area, yet I see it more with women, and especially with high-powered businesswomen. When they get stuck in this chakra, they wake up one day and say, "Oh my God. I'm forty and I don't know what happened. I don't know why there's not a man in my life. I want to have kids. Is it too late?"

Unblocking the Third Chakra

- Healing work

- Take a break and slow down

- Love something or somebody

- Feel emotions

- Quit your job and spend some of your savings

- Stop being willful

- Complete relationship with father

- Yoga

- Tai Chi

- Anything that brings awareness to the third chakra

Fran came to me with a major dilemma. She loved her job and the tons of money she earned, yet she was not happy. The accolades of being good at her work were very important to her, but her body was rebelling from all the stress. There was a fleeting hope of having a family; however, her biological clock was ticking at age forty-two. She wanted me to tell her if a family was in her future.

I was very careful with Fran, as she was looking for answers from me that could create a battle of wills if I did not say the right thing. I told her I would not play this game, and that she needed to get honest with herself. I said, "How important is money to you? What are you willing to sacrifice to have money?" The "voice" told me she was on her way to health problems if she did not disengage from the tornado of drama that typified her life. I told her as much, not to scare her, but to get her attention. We worked with her energy and opened her heart. At the core, there was a frightened little girl with a big heart. We cleared her fear of survival and made room for much more faith in her life. She decided to take up painting and yoga and cut back on her workload. She recently quit her job and has now taken up painting full-time. At last, she has made space in her life to have a life. It will not surprise me if a relationship does not enter her life soon.

Blocks to the Fourth Chakra

- Fear of receiving love

- Focus on giving love and care taking

- Fear of feeling love and opening up

- Tightness in the back of the heart

- Anxiety, heart palpitations

The heart is crucial to our health, well-being, and Spiritual evolution. The fear of receiving love is a problem common to most of us—it is easier to give love without the expectations that come from receiving it. When we give, we can stay in control. Opening your heart to receive creates a vulnerability that arises from an expectation of getting hurt; if you receive love, what will the person expect from you in return?

The fear of receiving love is often inherited from the father and passed on to the children; I suspect that this is the way men are wired. Traditionally focused on being providers and earning a living, they have not been as open to receive. Now I have a good intuition about clients who have lost their fathers to heart attacks. And why are men more subject to heart attacks than women? Because there is an energy block in the back of their hearts, blocking some of the sensitivity and vulnerability of receiving. Touch your dad between his shoulder blades—this is the Spiritual heart area. Massage this area, if he will let you, and say, "Dad, I love you. Let me in." See what happens.

Unblocking the Fourth Chakra

+ Healing work

+ Expose the fear around receiving love

+ Receive more love

+ Give less until you can receive more; balance

+ When there is balance, love more

+ Yoga

+ Sufi dance

+ Compassion

+ Meditation

+ Gratitude

+ Anything that brings awareness to the fourth chakra

Randy, a video editor, was in pain about a lost relationship. He was having anxiety and strange feelings in his heart. Although his doctor said he was fine physically, I could sense the grief around his heart; the tightness around his heart was due to blocks that he had in place to protect it from hurting. Originally these blocks may have acted as filters, keeping certain things out as well as limiting what comes in, and now it was time for the blocks to be released. When he breathed, his hands locked up and his forearms tightened. I could tell the back of his heart was blocked. We worked in that area and he started to cry. I had him say, "It is safe for me to receive love." He said his ex-girlfriend, Sharon, told him he would not let her in. The block (fear) in the back of his heart kept her out. The "voice" said the fear was something he inherited from his father. I asked, "Does your father have a heart problem?" Randy said that his father died of a heart attack when he (Randy) was a baby. Randy felt the energy of the block in his heart at that moment and was able to let it go; he did not need a heart attack to become aware of this limitation. His heart stayed open after our session, and he soon reconciled with Sharon, now able to let her in.

Blocks to the Fifth Chakra

- Fear of expressing yourself

- Holding back the voice

- Holding back opinions

- Sore throat, laryngitis

- Stiff neck (pain in the neck)

- Pinched nerve

- Choking feeling

My gift of Clairaudience is located in the fifth chakra. I feel many things through my throat, and I especially feel it when someone is afraid to use their throat to speak, or refuses to hear the truth. During breath work, many blocks and physical manifestations show up in the throat area. The lips and mouth can get very tight, making it difficult to speak, particularly for people who suppress their voice or their opinions. With some people, the throat may actually get a red band or stripe around it like an old scar. These are usually indicators of neck or throat trauma in a past life; hence, the hesitancy to fully express through the throat during this lifetime.

I try to stay focused on this lifetime because we can take responsibility for it; if there are very poignant past life memories, I bring those experiences to the present and deal with them until they are released. If someone is willing to do the work, they are ready to deal with the karmic pattern of past life experiences.

Unblocking the Fifth Chakra

- Healing work

- Speak up

- Express yourself artistically; sing or act

- Be a good listener

- Creativity, communication, healing

- Anything that brings awareness to the fifth chakra

At age thirty-nine, Tracy was a television writer who had trouble expressing herself. When she got very nervous, the blocks in her throat were easy to detect. Her voice would shake, I could see tension in her throat, and I felt vulnerability from her as she spoke. Tracy was moving up the ranks as a writer and was now pitching a show of her own. Luckily, she had a partner who would do the talking, as she could not speak at important meetings; she would actually lose her voice.

As we worked on this, abuse from her father emerged. When she was younger he would tell her to shut up, and to speak when spoken to. She had acquired a second-class quality that denied her power. She must have been meant to overcome this because we were working on it, and the universe had put her in the position where she had to use her voice. We found her voice during our work together. It was hard work, and as we cut through the energy of the suppression, her true voice came forth. In a short time, confidence started to flow through as she spoke. It was exciting to see her come into her power as a woman through the throat chakra. As the blocks cleared out of the throat, she connected to more creativity around her ovaries. It grounded her and her voice got deeper and more assured. Tracy has moved along in her career and is taking up directing, which will be a true test for her voice; now she is ready for it.

Blocks to the Sixth Chakra

- Fear to see the truth (psychically)

- Migraine headaches

- Need to make things linear or one-dimensional

- Need to understand everything intellectually

- Eye disorders, wandering eye, being cross-eyed

- Sugar addiction and deep-seated mother issues

People who are blocked in the sixth chakra may get intense headaches. They may also have pronounced wrinkles between the eyebrows because they try to force information to a place of intellectual understanding, rather than to a more universal understanding in the heart. Also, tension in the third eye region blocks psychic intuition. Sometimes that is why the tension is there, to act as a filter to keep a person from seeing the truth. It is safer to stay in a place of confusion, or a place of trying to understand, than the truth.

The eyes are called the windows of the soul. Much can be discerned about a person by studying the energy around their eyes and third eye center. Usually, the third eye can only open after the heart is opened. When the heart is open the head gets to relax, and when the head relaxes, the third eye can open.

Sixth chakra energy blocks may also be revealed by dark under-eye circles. This characteristic can reveal a sugar addiction and usually issues with the mother, and I use it as a way into a person's core issues. I may ask about their relationship with sugar, and then their relationship with their mom. I investigate this energy further as I look at the second chakra, and see if the person is blocked here. These factors are explored more with intuition than as blanket statements. In other words, they can be signs to watch for, but they are not absolutes.

Unblocking the Sixth Chakra

- Healing work

- Love

- Let go of the need to understand everything intellectually

- Trust your intuition to see for you

- Imagination

- Understand the phrase, "I see."

- Anything that brings awareness to the sixth chakra

Kelly, a twenty-eight-year-old actress, was extremely intelligent and equally intuitive. She was psychically tuned-in to more than she let on, and had a habit of pleading confusion much of the time. Her confusion was compounded around groups of people, even though she asked perceptive questions revealing to everyone how smart she was. She was killing her intuition with this act of confusion. I called it her "dumb act." She had a history of migraine headaches that I believe were tied into the denial of her intuition. When she came to me one day with a horrible migraine, I knew she was ready to deal with this block. As we confronted her act of confusion, some energy released around her third eye and her migraine started to go away. Kelly's vision opened and she felt her intuition go through the roof. It was intense dealing with it at first and she realized the origins of her fears. We worked with it and demystified the importance of her newly opened gift. She fully integrated the intuition into her life, and it has helped her acting career in numerous ways, as well as, helping her start a new business: she now has a burgeoning, highly successful tarot reading practice.

Blocks to the Seventh Chakra

+ Fear of letting go and connecting with life

+ Control issues

+ Inability to focus on the Light

+ Depression; feelings of being alone

+ Fear about having faith

+ Fear of what change, letting go, and having faith might bring

Blocks in the crown (see Figure 14) are not as physically manifested as in the other chakras; however, the blocks are just as powerful, if not more so. These blocks appear more energetic and psychic. A person may have huge issues around letting go and connecting with things outside of him or her, or letting go and allowing energy pass through as if he or she were simply a conduit. People may also have blocks around their faith, because they will not allow themselves to connect to the Light. In other words, these blocks have a tendency to cause a person to feel cut off, alone, and isolated from the wholeness and one-ness of life.

To Unblock the Seventh Chakra

+ Healing work

+ Do the exercises in the Pyramid of Life section

+ Connect to the stars, planets, sun, moon, and sky

+ Spiritual growth

+ Self-realization

+ Understand the phrase: "I am."

+ Universal oneness

+ Anything that brings awareness to the seventh chakra

Tom, a computer specialist, came to see me about his growing depression. Feeling isolated and alone, he did not feel con-nected to anything. I saw him as a sensitive soul and a com-puter brain. Could I lead Tom to some faith, or was he stuck in his ways? The "voice" told me he was angry with his father. He had a chip on his shoulder. I witnessed him coming into his Spiritual power and his connection with the oneness of the universe. He was ready for this healing and we joked about it being his mid-life crisis. We were able to pinpoint what was going on with Tom and deal with it directly. It was a beautiful thing to see him connect to Spirit and to his feel-ing about the world owing him something because his father was so tough on him as a kid. He was choosing to see himself as unsuccessful to get back at his father and his father's need for him to be successful. His underachieving kept his dad wor-rying about him.

As Tom began to believe his own act, depression set in and he found he could not get out of it. He grew cynical and he had no faith. I knew he would be a tough case because he was invested in his condition. The only approach was to be straightforward. I told him things just as I saw them, and we dealt with his chip. When we cleared the energy of anger and separation, I almost did not recognize him.

In conclusion, the chakra system is a great way to talk about energy, healing, and the body. It unifies and gives language to many esoteric terms. Everyone is different and some of us relate to these descriptions and ideas better than others.

Ultimately, it is the clarity with which we communicate our ideas about the mind, body, and Spirit connection that determines our effectiveness as healers, authors, and human beings. We need to have a basic understanding of the chakras to navigate the Spiritual path.

KUNDALINI

Described as a ball of fire or a snake that moves up the spine, kundalini is an Eastern term for the energy that releases from the sacrum and moves along the spine. I have felt this a few times myself and have witnessed it with several clients.

It is rather shocking to witness. When the energy starts to move, it may seem to be just sexual energy and the person may be acting a little dramatic. Yet, kundalini is far more than drama; it can appear very wild. The person may need to move their body, and the body will heat up and sweat, vibrate, emote, shake, sweat some more, and then relax into a deep state.

Many ask how they can experience kundalini. The easiest way is to use breath and to balance the chakra system. When the heart opens, energy starts to move through the body. If the body is open enough and you are able to connect to your chakras, the kundalini will move. This is very Spirit-related. When you invite in change, Spirit will deliver. This is especially true when the chakras are balanced and the heart is open. To move the kundalini up the spine and out the top of the head is a process where you learn to sustain the energy flow. This may occur during healing work, yoga, sex, meditation, birth, or death. The choice to work with and move the kundalini is a powerful choice in your life.

A medical student named Janet came to see me to learn more about Spirituality. She was very open in her chakras. When she started to breathe I could tell she was in for a wild ride— she had no fear and very few blocks. Right away her energy started to spin through the chakras. Her emotions cleared, she let out a scream, and her body started to vibrate and gyrate almost off the table, hitting a very deep state of aware-ness in her body. She started seeing a spinning golden ball of light above her head. This ball started shooting golden light down into her crown chakra just as her base released a ball of fire that started up the spine. She described the two balls of light meeting in her heart chakra. Janice said her soul merged inside her heart, then the light proceeded out the top of her head and back in, all the way down to her feet; the energy released down into the earth and back up again. It seemed to her that it could have gone on forever. Janet made powerful contact with her Spirit that day and it will stay with her for the rest of her life.

MEDITATION

Many people find it difficult to meditate. Our computer- and MTV-stimulated minds are going so fast that it seems almost impos-sible to slow down. It is not impossible, just almost impossible.

Although slowing down would benefit most people, I doubt it is possible for most. While we are inherently Spiritual beings, many of us have neither the time nor the desire to connect with our Spiritual side. More importantly, we may not have the desire to confront the things, such as fears, that block this connection. While this is a function of where we are as a society, there are exceptions. If you are reading this book, you may be an excep-tion. If you are reading this and experiencing an impact, we may be preparing another healer to go out into the world.

How do we get meditation to work for more people, particularly for those who are interested, yet just can't seem to do it? I suggest using the breath. The breath relaxes the brain and takes people to a meditative state easier than any other method. We need easy ways to make contact with our Spiritual side, accessible ways for people to experience Spiritual concepts. Some may sit in silence for days or go to the desert to find peace, and others just cannot.

My views on meditation are liberal. I am interested in getting people to a place where they disengage from the machine they believe to be the real world. I do the best I can to slow them down for a few minutes and get them to step outside the chasm of their lives. For some people, the starting point may be a hike, a swim, a massage, arts and crafts, or gardening. Once they slow down, we have a chance; and, if they do the healing work, they realize how seduced they are by the illusions they have about life. All they may see are their mortgage payments, taxes, insurance, credit cards, or hipster lifestyles. If they are staring at such a mountain of stress and responsibility, can healing work and meditation sink in?

I take whatever I can get. If I get only one chance with a client because someone dragged them to see me, I take it. God is orchestrating the work—I just get out of the way. If a person takes one hour out of their busy schedule, their life may be changed.

Once the seed is planted—even just a tiny mustard seed of truth—it can move mountains. In one peaceful, open, meditative moment, God can enter the mind, the body, and the consciousness, into the gap between the conscious mind and the expansive open mind and then into the Light. The meditative state is the key to this experience.

Mathew was an emergency room doctor who needed to disengage from the stress of his job. He was skeptical about healing and meditation work, but decided to give it a try; he was a natural. Ten minutes of breathing and he was ecstatic. The stress released out of his body and he completely recharged

himself in a matter of a few minutes. He comes in now for a
tune-up every few weeks.

YOGA

Yoga is another philosophy that originated in the East and is
now highly popular in the West. I believe yoga is popular because
it is both physical and Spiritual, and has proven to be healing,
engaging our bodies and our minds through the physical.

Yoga is an active meditation, just like the breath work. As
healings and openings occur, it is important to have a healthy,
open spine. Yoga helps with the process of opening and letting
the Light and energy pass through the spine, to connect to more
Light, to align and heal the spine.

With yoga you can release and move through physical and
intellectual resistance. It is a tool to bring in the Light. The breath
is a large part of yoga practice. Clearing the body with this
method prepares us for future journeys with our consciousness.

I do not know what the specifics of these future journeys
will be just yet; however, I can tell you that a journey is in store
for all of us. Is it in addition to death, or beyond that? We are
poised to see and experience big changes in our lifetime—the
world is evolving that fast. Use yoga to prepare yourself, to
ground and to open yourself for clarity.

If you choose love as your beacon, the lighthouse will always
remain in view and you will be able to navigate through the
labyrinth of illusions of the physical world. Our bodies and
minds can be this labyrinth of illusion. Using yoga can help
streamline and align the energy outside and within our bodies
to help us know who we are. Yoga helps fine-tune our connection with the flow of energy.

I find a Spiritual flow in all of the exercise I do, including
basketball, mountain biking, spinning and yoga. A true yogi will
tell you that yoga practice is for the mind, body, and soul, and I
believe it is. Give yoga a try and see what it can do for you. Be
aware that there are many flavors of yoga practice, which vary by
discipline, class structure and amount of physical exertion. Try

several types and see which philosophy and physical regimen works for you. An instructor will prove to be equally important to your development. Just do it—I cannot stress this enough. And for those of you who already practice yoga, keep it up.

I currently do not practice yoga with a teacher. I check in with my body and see where it needs attention and energy. I set aside time for a mini yoga class ten to fifteen minutes a day, working or stretching the tight areas. In the healing work I practice pranayama yoga with the breath exercise, so I get in a fair amount of yoga each day. My body has been asking for more yoga exercise so I will be increasing it to twenty to thirty minutes per day. My physical yoga practice is a blend of Bikram's, kundalini, and Hatha yoga, the types for which I have the most affinity.

CHAPTER SEVEN

LIFE FORCE ENERGY

Now we focus on sun, gardening and agriculture. Healing is about awareness, and my awareness is greatly affected by my connection to the earth, and the earth's connection to the sun. The earth and sun keep us alive. I pay close attention to growing and eating my own food. It is all connected.

We are responsible for our state of affairs, and knowledge about gardening and agriculture is as important as knowledge about the stock market or knowledge about chakras. If you can harvest new understanding of the life force from the information herein, it may help you expand and have appreciation for what sustains you.

I believe healing comes from knowledge and instinctive intuition; to say we are what we eat is an understatement. You do not need to be super conscious to eat fast food; as a matter of fact, you may be unconscious when you put that kind of non-nourishment into your body. We are a society of convenience, which breeds complacency, lack of involvement, and patronization by the public sector. If the demand for organic foods continues to grow, then agriculture and food service industries will be forced to respond. Some fast-food establishments are beginning to recognize this. Fast-food restaurants are offering veggie burgers, turkey burgers, Atkins diet sandwiches, and wider arrays of salads. I expect to see a chain of fast, healthy food restaurants with drive-through windows, and I know they would do well in many cities, especially Los Angeles.

THE SUN

Most ancient cultures had religions and beliefs related to the sun. They recognized it as the source of the Light. We are here because of the unceasing energy of the sun—it is always working, burning, glowing and illuminating our planet and our solar system. Do you stop and give praise to the sun or do you take it for granted?

Many Spiritual teachings, dogmas, and words are metaphors for the sun:

+ The Father and the Son/sun

+ The Light

+ White-gold light

+ Sun salutations

+ Radiation

+ Photosynthesis

+ Enlightened

+ Ra, the Sun God

When you are lost and have nothing to worship or observe, pay attention to the sun. It was the beginning and will have something to do with the end. And what do I mean by "the end?" There could be a shift or change in the sun's temperature or quality of light. I hope this does not happen, yet I know the sun holds the key to many principles about why we are here. Science is doing its best to explain the relationship of the earth to the sun and the development of life here on earth. I believe the earth and everything on it is an intentional community created and watched over by higher beings, and that we are here for a reason, with all life forms being part of this grand experiment. Within this experiment, the earth and the sun are key players. The ancient ones knew the importance of this connection; people today have been removed from the acknowledgment of why we are here, how we are here, and how we survive. The sun is the center of our universe. I am not telling you to go to Egypt and worship the sun; however, it may be good to look at your relationship to the sun.

I am not afraid of the sun's rays. Being afraid of the sun may be an illusion marketed by pharmaceutical companies and dermatologists. I'm not trying to convince the allopathic community of anything—their business is built on creating demand for their business. Finding our individual truth about our body's ability to heal and stay healthy is our own responsibility, and I do not give that power to a doctor. The relationship I live with is most alive and vital when I embrace the sun. I am not suggesting that you bake in the sun, nor lather on sunscreen. I prefer to get some sun and then get out of its direct light in the heat of the day. I do not like or trust how sunscreen feels on my body.

THE SUN EXERCISE

Look at the sun just before sunset. If your eyes will allow you to stare at it for a few moments, do so. Let the light and the heat warm up your third eye. Receive the light, let it awaken your vision. Close your eyes after a few moments and allow your mind's eye to continue to see the light. Embrace the soft, golden white light of the setting sun. It is very healing for your soul, as well as your crown, third eye, throat, heart, solar plexus, pelvis, and base chakras. Keep focused on the light. It will not steer you the wrong way.

We are being socially conditioned to look at the sun as a detriment. Yet, the sun is responsible for everything that grows and everything we eat. Let us not take it for granted. Appreciate the sun for its healing qualities in a healing way and give it the respect it deserves. The sun heals us by feeding everything that feeds us. Do not underestimate the healing properties of the sun. The sun's heat and light is the most important energy we will ever feel; without it we are dead.

GARDENING

One of the most basic forms of healing and survival, gardening is also one of the most Spiritual things I do. It connects me with Mother Earth, the plant and animal kingdoms, and to all nature. Gardening teaches me to be creative with forces outside myself. I listen to and connect with the soil to see what it needs to be brought into balance, to see where certain plants want to grow and which ones are compatible, and how much room they need. To do this, I step back from the picture I see in front of me and connect to the potential of this piece of earth. (The same way I look at the potential with people.)

It heals me when I am in sync with nature. When we show respect, nature's greatest desire is to please us. I love helping plants grow and watching them respond to tender loving care. I am energized when I harvest my own food, wash it, and eat it. Wherever I am living, I try to establish an organic garden. If I am restricted to a pot and a tiny bit of sunlight, I can still grow herbs and tomatoes. I like to have a kitchen garden as close to the house as possible, so I can just pick something, wash, and eat it. In cities like Los Angeles, I place gardens wherever I can make them work. I usually grow tomatoes, cucumbers, squash, onions, carrots, beets, spinach, lettuce, kale, collards, broccoli, basil, rosemary, and corn. It all depends on how much space I have and the season.

Why is gardening so healing for me? My granddad was an amazing gardener. I come from a long line of farmers, so it helps connect me with my roots. I am healed when I grow healthy plants with full consciousness. Plants respond to nurturing and love just like people do; there is no difference, just a different language. When I set up an organic garden, I do several things:

+ Determine a good, sunny location, as most vegetables need plenty of sunlight.

+ Next, I check the soil to determine if it is alive or whether it has been traumatized or neglected. I work it, touch it, feel it, water it, and see what it needs intuitively.

+ I feed the soil with homemade compost made from organic matter, which is live soil—plants love it. I use earthworms to recycle leaves, weeds, straw, scraps, and horse manure into compost and I encourage the earthworms to visit the garden, too. This is accomplished as I transfer the compost, full of earthworms, to the garden; I allow them to migrate. As long as there is organic matter for worms to eat, they live and travel through the soil, breaking down matter into digestible food for plants. Worms rehabilitate the soil and create new soil.

+ I balance the soil and compost with biodynamic remedies. These are homeopathic-like solutions developed to free the natural properties of the soil. These solutions come from the teachings of Rudolph Steiner, the creator of the Waldorf Schools. He was clairvoyant and created this information from a channeling he did in the late 1800s. He believed the soil was a living organism and was very much a part of the Spiritual world. Opposing the popular view from the scientific community that the soil was dead, he created a practice of Spiritual sciences called anthroposophy, which I find fascinating and helpful in reclaiming diseased and damaged soils. There are also a number of remedies called Biodynamic Preparations, available through the Josephine Porter Institute at www.jpibiodynamics.org.

- ◆ I set up a watering drip system for each plant, to minimize water waste.

- ◆ When I plant a seed or transplant a plant, I hold each in my hand and focus intention on it with visual images to show the plant or seeds that I recognize their full potential.

- ◆ I mulch the plants with straw to keep in moisture, keep out weeds, and build organic matter.

- ◆ I playfully set intention for the whole garden, asking the elf and fairy kingdom to watch over my garden and make it a magical playground. I do this with the child-like part of my imagination, finding some areas where these entities can play, such as a fountain, around some rocks, or under the tomatoes. When I leave for an extended time period, I verbally ask the elves and fairies to keep an eye on things and I let them know that it is okay for nature to take the last part of each row or ten percent of the crop. We all share. As they grow and mature, plants need very little. Healthy, vigorous plants rarely have problems with insects or disease.

I like taking a diseased piece of land and healing it, bringing it back to life. Soil contracts and shuts down when it is neglected and abused, just like people do. The key is to tune into the soil and convince it that it is safe to come out of dormancy and live again. You can rejuvenate soil by holding it like you would a person's hand. Work the soil with the intention that it will heal and grow healthy plants. Time and time again I have seen the worst soils healed in a very short time with these methods.

Everything in the plant world starts with the soil. Once I get it breathing, growing plants is a breeze. Like the body, once we get it balanced, a person usually does just fine. Healing works the same whether in soil, plants, animals or people. Where awareness goes, energy flows.

AGRICULTURE

My granddad told me, "Once farmers in this county were held in high esteem. They fed themselves and their neighbors. Now, farmers are looked at and treated like second-class citizens. One of these days when most farmers have left their farms, when there is not enough food and people get hungry, look out. When people have to pay $10 for a loaf of white bread, watch how things will change."

I do believe we are spoiled in this country. The small family farm is nearly extinct. Successful agriculture is huge and corporate. Economies of scale have hit agriculture, similar to how Wal-Marts can wipe out many small community businesses. The risks to the consumer of products from such large-scale operations come down to dependence on a few sources for our food supply. As we have homogenized our plant genetics there is greater risks to widespread disease and failure. Science can sometimes get ahead of itself when it comes to nature, and genetic engineering may prove to be a prime example. With these practices, the focus is on maximum production. We must produce, produce, produce to feed this country and the world. What we are seeing is more science, refinement, and processing, and less vitality, taste, and nutrition in our food. It has taken a while to figure out that white sugar, white flour, and white salt are diluted versions of their stalwart predecessors cane sugar, whole wheat flour, and mineral salt. Look at how popular the return to the old ways is growing. People are proving their loyalty with the exploding organic food market. How often do you pour white sugar on your cereal, or ask for a sandwich on white bread?

The small farmers who hold out must keep up with the latest trends and technology to compete with the corporate operations. The corporate agricultural machine is well oiled. Farmers have increased productivity to the maximum with synthetic fertilizers, herbicides (weed killers), pesticides (pest killers), and hybridization of plant varieties.

Today, science develops plants that are genetically altered so that they are more tolerant of chemicals and more resistant to insects and disease. What we end up with are foods we cannot trust. As a response, you have people who want naturally produced foods and are willing to pay for them.

Livestock consumes much of the genetically altered food in their feed such as corn and soybeans, and the beef, chickens, and pork are making their way to our dinner tables. Genetically altered ingredients are also used in processed foods, where they can be hidden or blended in as minor items. Many foreign countries are having a problem with the use of genetically altered plants. If widespread boycotting continues, it may slow the promotion of this technology. Why am I so concerned about all of the science affecting our sustenance? Here are some of the reasons:

- Uniform hybridization of all the major crops could expose the crops to a genetic defect, resulting in widespread disease wiping out the surplus of our food resources. If all the plants are the same or closely-related, they lose diversity and the ability to withstand such attack.

- Gene altering is moving farmers farther away from the Spiritual practice of growing what they need to survive. It is making farming a monitored, scientific process that is dependent on synthetic chemicals and fertilizers.

- We are being pressured to grow more food to feed the world. It is a catch-22.

I wholly support organic foods because they have more vitality, energy, and nutrients than conventionally grown foods. Even though conventionally grown produce is bigger, brighter, and more perfectly uniform, it lacks taste and nutrients due to the use of nitrogen fertilizer. As steroids do on the human body, nitrogen causes the plants to grow bigger than organic plants; the end result is plants and fruits that are swollen with more water, which dilutes the taste and nutrients.

When growing conditions are right for plants, they grow. Insects avoid healthy, vigorous plants. They attack and destroy unhealthy plants, so the need for pesticides is usually due to unhealthy plants and unfavorable growing conditions. The use of herbicides allows farmers to kill and control weeds more easily. These chemicals are generally thought to be less harmful than pesticides, although they are now proving to be just as deadly and toxic.

Herbicides have made their way into water systems, and between pesticides, herbicides, petrochemicals, industrial waste, radioactive waste, and chemicals, an untainted water supply these days is rare.

The agricultural machine is so huge, we will never be an organic nation or world, yet you and I can help. The more consciousness we bring to reclaiming the health of Mother Earth, the better off we all are. What we put in our bodies has a cumulative effect, and at some point, our bodies will no longer tolerate junk food, the same way Mother Earth will no longer tolerate being abused and poisoned.

That is a prediction, and I believe the day is coming when the earth will not accept any more abuse. Humans take too much for granted; we feel entitled to use the earth, to mine her resources. The earth is a living entity. Resources including plants and animals may be here to provide us with certain comforts, but nothing on the earth is here for us to abuse. I am not sold on our ability to manipulate and do as we please with the earth and her natural resources. I believe Mother Nature is going to teach humankind some lessons about respect very soon, unless we learn to reconnect to nature, the land, and its resources. Farmers who love, respect, and protect the land are part of her natural resources. The guardians, custodians, and stewards of the earth must step forward soon.

Granddad said the farmers would be needed one day and they would be held in high esteem. "Just wait to see what happens when people get hungry," he said. "You will see that in your lifetime." My granddad seemed to be making the same prediction as I am today.

It is important for everyone to have a garden, to grow some of the foods we eat, and to get familiar with seeds, plants, and the soil. You may have a little yard space, a flowerbed, a sunporch, a patio or at least a window with some good sun. Grow some herbs on the windowsill, a tomato plant in a pot, or a flower. You may not have the time, or a green thumb; nevertheless, you will be healthier and will find it healing to grow your own food.

At fifty-eight, Victor left the corporate world because of his failing health. Doctors did not know what was wrong, although they did tell him he was not handling stress well. He decided that the problem was his job, so he retired early and moved to the country. To return to his roots, he planted a garden, a large garden, because he had the time and space for it. The produce allowed him to connect with his neighbors as he gave food away to all of them. Within the first year of retirement, Victor felt better than he had in twenty years. He started making birdhouses and custom signs in his woodworking shop when he was not gardening. He won several vegetable contests at the local fair. His wife says he is a new man in more ways than one. Victor healed his unexplained condition using his hands and connecting to the earth with his gardening.

In defense of modern agriculture, technology and science provide us with tremendous opportunities to feed the world— today's small farmers and corporate operations do produce an abundance of food. Nonetheless, farmland in this country dwindles every day as commercial and residential development takes over. As it turns out, we need technology to feed us.

Americans are fortunate to have the choices we do around our food sources. If we want to eat organically and more healthfully, we can. We have many more choices than people in developing countries.

If you remember my roots, that I am from a farm and the land, you can see how this discussion of food and agriculture belong in the book; roots are powerful.

CHAPTER EIGHT

SEXUALITY AND THE SECOND CHAKRA

How much clarity do you have around your sexuality? This is traditionally such a taboo subject that most people find it difficult to discuss honest motivations around the topic. Let us lay the groundwork to discuss sexuality by defining a few terms. Most of this chapter deals with sexual abuse.

SEXUALITY

Sexuality is the connection to, and expression of, your life force. It can involve sexual appeal or interest in sexual activity. When sexuality is healthy and flows as a creative force, it results in joy, artistic expression, self-love, empowerment, pregnancy, and freedom. It is a reflection of your celebration of life. When it is not healthy, the flow may be distorted by judgment, desires, manipulation, seduction, confusion, and other negative intentions, and abuse may result.

SEX

Sex is about sexual activity or behavior leading to it. Sex can be an act of love, yet as we all know, sex often occurs without love—it can just be about hooking up or sexual intercourse. I want to distinguish between sex and sexuality. Just because you are in touch with your sexuality does not mean that you want to have sex. It is not an open invitation. Having sex should involve choice and agreement from both or all sides.

NUDITY

Nudity is the state of having no clothes on. It does not equal sexuality and sexuality does not equal sex. In other words, when you choose to be nude, it is not the full expression of your sexuality and it does not mean that you want to have sex. That is the liberating offer of nudism. If you have ever visited a nude beach you may have experienced strange feelings at first. Once you realize there is not a massive orgy taking place, you may start to relax and enjoy the liberation of the experience. You see how people express themselves without hiding behind clothes. It is worth the experience if you can confront it. Of course, this is old news in much of the world.

PREDATOR

A predator is an energy, person, family, or group that takes from others, or destroys others for gain. A sexual predator uses sexual energy to accomplish this. I often refer to this energy as a dark energy.

SEXUAL ABUSE

Sexual abuse happens when sexual energy is used to take clarity, energy, and control away from a victim. It is carried and perpetuated by a predator type of energy. This energy can be a person, family, or group. The predator is compelled to use sexual energy to possess and dominate a weaker victim. Predators are skilled and often aggressive, determined, and persistent about their intent to abuse sexually. With this skill and focus, the second chakra—"love of power"—is the easiest way for the predator to enter another person's energy field.

SEXUAL ABUSE EXPOSED

Predators are bringing attention to the fact that society tends to ignore human rights in the sexual area, particularly human rights for women. The issue is an emotional powder keg, making it difficult for you to be objective, as it has in the past been a closed subject. Nonetheless, consciousness has a way of cutting through illusion. It is time to get clear about our energy and boundaries. This will help all of us, and as a result, we will all experience more personal power.

Sexual abuse is a hot topic in the world, exposed and confronted more today than at any other time in our history. People are speaking up about being abused, courts are prosecuting abusers, the media is communicating the stories, and secrets are being revealed. The Catholic Church is an organization that has been greatly affected by these developments. They have spent millions of dollars to fight and settle court cases. The Church is realizing that abuse problems cannot be swept under the rug anymore. Of course this is not limited to the Catholic Church, for this has been present for eons in places where there is abuse of power, authority, and control. Examples can be found in a variety of areas: families, the poor, the wealthy, immigrants, politics and politicians, military, wars, education and schools, corporations, sports teams, Hollywood, and the entertainment business, to name a few.

Most of us are mesmerized and shocked by the sensationalism in the media surrounding sexual abuse. The world is a media-based arena and if abuse makes the headlines, we see or hear about it. The abused people who are speaking up and exposing the abusers has put an element of fear into the life of the abuser. The exposure is bringing out more information about the darker, illicit activities that go on in the underground world of sex slaves, bondage, and the prostitution of children. People do not want to know about the worst of it, and this is why it has remained taboo throughout time. In any case, too many people, especially women and children, are still being abused today.

I believe something is happening with human consciousness that is bringing awareness to this abuse. More people are taking a stand for what is right, and humanity is intensely looking into human rights around this issue. As a collective body, we are limited in consciousness to the level of those being abused (if we do not take a stand for them). In other words, if we continue to sweep it under the rug, we will be trapped under the rug as well. Looking the other way does not keep us pure, especially if we know what is going on.

BREAKING IT DOWN

In healing work, I deal with the energy around sexual abuse. When people come to me, they have generally explored this in therapy or have been seeking help for it for years. I seem to be the last stop. They are seeking help to clear the energy, and several therapists have sent clients to me for this specific reason. What is sexual abuse to one person might not be to another person; if a person is blocked, traumatized, in pain, or reliving the experience, then it was abuse to them and needs healing. Sexual abuse energy can get stuck within the physical, emotional, mental, and Spiritual levels in a person's consciousness. Sexual abuse is not just physical.

For example, Leslie had many experiences of being abused by two older stepbrothers, who harassed her for years. She worked on this for over ten years in therapy. It started when she was three and her mom remarried; suddenly she acquired two stepbrothers, seven and nine years old. They beat her (physical), teased her (emotional), manipulated her from telling on them (mental), and kept her in a constant state of fear throughout her early life (Spiritual). Leslie said much of it was sexual abuse. She remembers being groped, fondled, and having oral sex. When she was twelve, she told her mom (Pam) and stepfather (Bob), and they did not believe her stories. Leslie thought her mom was afraid to stand up for her because she would have to disapprove of the boys. Leslie moved away from home when she was sixteen.

Physical sexual abuse is the most commonly talked-about sexual abuse, but I look at how sexual energy can penetrate other levels, too. The other levels (emotional, mental, and Spiritual) can take on a psychic quality, and I refer to them collectively as psychic sexual abuse. In the psychic realm and in a non-physical way, the sexual energy gets woven into the matrix of who a person thinks they are, and it can hardly be detected or cleared. It is extremely tricky energy, very snake-like, and with the ability to camouflage itself very discreetly. In Leslie's case, she came to me confused about her personal space and boundaries. She had problems with men other than her brothers. Relationships were revolving doors with her. She wanted help clearing sexual abuse out of her space completely. She asked, "Is there something in me that keeps attracting these experiences? Is there something wrong with me?"

Leslie's family disowned her years ago and wanted no part of her story. They were furious when she told a social worker of her abuse, bringing embarrassment to the family. The authorities ultimately believed the family, who claimed that she was the problem, not the boys. She was programmed to think she was crazy and it had a strong psychic effect on her.

These scenarios are always complex, and the complexity does not help in sorting through the details to find a way to help a person. Leslie's situation is mild compared to many. Can she be healed enough to move on with her life? Why has she magnetized this abuse and deceit in her life? What is the lesson in this for her? Will she "get" it?

I have seen Leslie make tremendous growth in the recovery of her life. She is becoming clear that there is nothing wrong with her. Occasionally she will regress and become abusive to herself; she had a problem with drugs and depression. These energies are powerfully seductive and dark. I believe she will make it through this trauma because she has a huge appetite for life and she has shown aptitude for the bigger picture. Beginning the healing process within herself, every day she is letting go of the abusers more and she is getting the lessons for herself. She is learning to love and trust herself, learning to trust her own male energy and making friends with men before getting involved with them. Ultimately, Leslie is making peace within herself and finding her connection to God.

PSYCHIC SEXUAL ABUSE

Psychic sexual abuse is seductive because it is about "the love of power." Predators who abuse this way are usually trying to recapture energy that was once taken from them. When the abused becomes the abuser, it becomes a perpetual cycle. Psychic sexual abuse often happens in addition to the physical sexual abuse, or can happen independently of it. In other words, a predator may be using sexual energy to control someone through emotional, mental, Spiritual ways. In Leslie's case, this would have been the teasing, threatening, controlling, and suppressing, even after the boys quit molesting her.

At the core of it, Leslie never felt safe with her stepfather. She felt her mom was controlled by some dark sexual energy from this man. Pam had many problems and never recovered from the loss of her first marriage. She did not want to be alone and married Bob after knowing him just a few weeks. Leslie said Bob approved of his sons' abuse of her. He always said, "My fine sons would never abuse anyone." To the best of her recollection Bob never touched her sexually, yet she never felt safe around him. She would catch him looking at her in a strange way, and she always felt creepy if he ever touched her at all. She left home at sixteen because she felt less safe around him than the sons. As she got older, she could see the dynamic that controlled and held her mom to this man. Pam was afraid of him, and she was addicted to him sexually.

Leslie started to realize that she was not crazy, which she had been inclined to think about herself. The twisted energy with her family had almost succeeded in convincing her of this. She was on her own with this abuse most of her life. As she started to talk about it, her family resented her more. The distortion and spinning tornado of confusion, anger, and sexual energy that had entered her second chakra was a powerful magnet that attracted most of the abuse in her life.

Leslie realized that she inherited a strong imprint of abuse from her mom. She continually asked, "Why did this happen to me? Why me? Did I really need these lessons? Would I have experienced this if my mom had not remarried?"

At least Leslie was aware from an early age that something was wrong with the picture. Leaving home at sixteen was diffi cult, but she got out. Some people do not get out. Many people have blocked the memories around all types of abuse. If they do not remember it, they do not have to confront trying to under-stand it, and understanding sexual abuse is tricky at best.

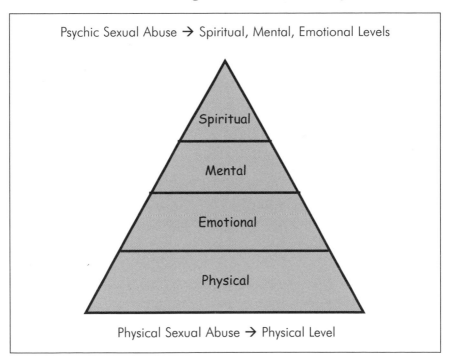

Psychic Sexual Abuse → Spiritual, Mental, Emotional Levels

Spiritual

Mental

Emotional

Physical

Physical Sexual Abuse → Physical Level

Figure 15. Sexual Abuse and the Pyramid of Life

How do you acknowledge sexual abuse if you were never touched or violated physically?

Mandy, a thirty-five-year-old hair stylist, is sure she has never been sexually abused on a physical level. However, her thera- pist and several people over the years told her they are sure she has been. As Mandy has a good memory of her life, it is frus- trating for her to hear these things and not be able to connect them to any experiences. She said it might have been easier if something had happened physically so she could connect it.

Many women come to me with similar stories; they also have constipation problems, a low sex drive, feelings of extreme vul- nerability around sex with their partners, and recurring dreams of being abused. Basically they feel shut down or disempowered around sex. If these problems are not due to physical sexual abuse, what are they due to? On an individual basis there could be different emotional, mental, or Spiritual reasons, but I am speaking of cases where people have explored all the options. For many, I am the last stop. They have done therapy, hor- mones, antidepressants, diets, bodywork, and more therapy. They cannot connect the dots, they cannot clear the energy that is causing the disturbance.

CLEARING SEXUAL ABUSE

We work with the energetic blockages in their bodies, and as we clear the blockages people start to get back into their bodies. The energy starts to flow and healing occurs. Psychic sexual energy is subtle, well camouflaged, and elusive. I sense it by the way a client's energy does or does not flow through the body, especially the pelvis. If sexual abuse energy is pres- ent, the area may be very sensitive or even ticklish to touch. Most people carry some sort of sexual abuse in their body. I encourage them to release any fear, confusion, emotions, memories, or blocks out of their body. By noticing the ener- gy, you can start working with it through your awareness. Where awareness goes energy flows.

The first time I worked with Leslie, I noticed an outwardly sexual, seductive quality about her. The "voice" told me the sexual energy she carried was not all hers. It was a spinning mass of energy that felt like a tornado around her, with a lot of emotional volatility in it. Once I let her know I could see through this and that this energy was not her, the whole house of cards came tumbling down. As I worked with the energies, her body sent out waves of sexual energy trying to stimulate or seduce me. As I immediately and verbally acknowledged each flow of energy, it dissolved. If it had hooked me, the work would have stopped with this energy taking over the session. (Getting hooked could result in confusion or temporary loss of focus. It only takes a second for this energy to take over.)

As I brought awareness to the energy by focusing on it and asking questions, it started to release; however, it was very crafty, and gave the illusion that it was cleared when it was not. I had to focus like a laser. I showed Leslie how the energy worked through her and tried to stay in possession of her. As the energy would come up, she would get seduced by it, just as her mom was addicted to it in Bob. Leslie was addicted to the way sexual energy moved through her. It turned her on in a sexual way and had the power to keep her trapped in second chakra reality. I know this may sound like *The Exorcist* and on some level it is, just not as obviously dramatic. Eventually, as we got more awareness to her about these abused energies, we were able to clear them.

To give you an example of the power and magnitude of sexual abuse energy, I describe sexual abuse, heroin addiction, and manic depression as three of the most powerful energies that affect humans. They seem to be related and hide within a dark black energy cloud. Seductive, they can take on a type of "possession" quality. Sexual abuse energy has the ability to work through a person and they never know the energy is not from within. It is a master parasite.

ARE YOU A PREDATOR?

As most of us carry a little sexual abuse energy, are we all predators to some degree? Have you ever found yourself trying to control or dominate a weaker individual? If you know you have been abused sexually, you may have had more than one strange, complicated feeling flow through you sexually. I do not think most people are predators; however, some predator energy may well flow through you, creating confusion or blockages in your second chakra. Again, choice always comes into play around the actions we take.

Our social system is more interested in the predators who physically abuse people. I agree it is important to be handling this, and I am equally interested in the predator energy (dark energy), the psychic sexual parasitic energy that takes energy from others. Once more light is brought to this energy to illuminate its seductive web of power and to disarm its control of innocent victims, the world will be a different place. The important point is to provide people the opportunity to choose what their experiences are without being controlled by a dark energy.

Once we get energy flowing, stagnant energies release and move on. After releasing these energies a person usually has to urinate, which helps clear the energy physically. Some women have started menstruating right after these clearings.

Getting trapped by a predator takes only a second to establish a seductive connection. It can be a look, a wink, a lewd gesture, a light touch or a sexual touch. Predators are highly skilled and take the upper hand because they are operating in a Spiritual-like realm. A predator spots the weakness and plays the role of an authority figure, or someone with power. Many times I have heard a victim repeat this common line used by predators: "No one will ever love you like I do." The connection is shrouded with illusion, appears as love, and is very drug-like because the abused person is looking for love. Experiencing a cloud of confusion because of the illusion, and tempted by love, the victim agrees on some level to the pact. Sometimes the secrecy is never broken and the control lives on. It makes no sense that an abused person is attracting this abuse, yet from a soul level, it makes complete sense. You attract what you need to learn.

KARMA AND SEX

I believe in destiny, and that on the soul level, you have already agreed to the events that happen in this lifetime. Sexual abuse incidents could be connected to a predator energy that has been following you around for several lifetimes.

Andi, a thirty-five-year-old writer, always had a panicky feeling that she would never find love. Her panic was reinforced when she met Jesse and had a distinct feeling about knowing him before. They hooked up at a bar and he seduced her immediately. Andi said she had no willpower with him. A cold chill went up her spine when he looked at her. Even though he forcibly raped her in the parking lot, it was the best sex she ever experienced; sex was her drug with him.

Jesse had been in and out of prison and was involved with crystal meth when she met him. She knew he was trouble the second their eyes met, yet she was drawn to him like a moth to a flame. There was never a peaceful moment in her two weeks with him. Andi realized there was something between them beyond the power of this lifetime. She prayed for clarity and remembered that Jesse was in a recurring dream she had been having for years. As fast as he came, he was gone. Luckily for her, Jesse was incarcerated before they had time to recreate any past life experiences. This could never be proven to be true scientifically, yet each time I come into contact with a person with a lesson for me from my past life experiences always gives me a cold chill. Clients have made comments to me about being hooked by a person and their energy, and feeling helpless, as if they have no willpower. In Andi's case, she is certain there were previous lifetimes at play with her and Jesse.

I do not mean to scare you. If all this talk about sexual abuse irritates you or makes your head spin, refer to the next section in this chapter, Second Chakra Clearing Formula. There is a good chance you may be carrying some sexual abuse energy that needs clearing. I believe there is Spiritual karma at play here, that is, the eternal search for love from an outside source. I believe the soul of the abused knows abuse is coming and is actually looking for the connection to help them work something out within their belief system around love.

The question is, how long will it take the abused person to become aware of the abuse energy and disengage from it or get the lesson? The energy is not love, although it may feel like love at the time of the encounter with the predator. Why does the soul of an abused person enter into an agreement with this energy? This is where the outrage lies here on the earth plane. We are looking at the abused as lacking in free will. They are victims, at least physically. In the Spiritual realm they have chosen this engagement. Freedom does not come from trying to gain sympathy for being abused. Freedom comes from getting the lesson and making the connection on a karmic plane. Why did your soul come together with this other person? How long do you need to believe it was a random accident? The teaching never stops in the rhythm of life. I have worked with too many people who have been abused to believe there is any randomness to it.

> *Denise, a thirty-six-year-old music executive, came to me with huge abuse problems and issues. She had been raped and sexually assaulted many times. The energy was so strong around her you could feel it as soon as you heard her voice on the phone. Denise said she could be at a party or event with hundreds of people and the one sexual predator could spot her and would be harassing her within seconds.*

So this got me thinking about how insects spot sick plants with their infrared vision and go right to that plant to destroy it. Is there something like this going on with a predator? How are they led to the victims? How do they spot them in a crowd? Is karma creating something like an infrared signal? I believe a predator can spot sexual abuse energy; it emits a sexual tone, vibration, and feeling. They know the victim has no real boundaries to this energy, and they have the magic password. They know how to move energy in a seductive, Spiritually enhanced way. To repeat, it is disguised as LOVE.

In the Spiritual realm, there is karma, whether we want to acknowledge it or not. Abuse is wrong and perpetrators should be exposed. The information I am sharing here has to do with understanding their actions and the response of the victim to them, especially if you are someone who has been abused. I want to help you clear away unwanted energies. Clear away the drama and confusion, clear away the constipation of energy and bring light to old lessons that you no longer need in your space.

MOTIVATIONS AROUND SEXUAL ENERGY

So many people in our country are conservative, judgmental, and repressed around the subject of sexuality, it is no wonder that sex is an exploited subject. When conservative religious organizations try to control views about sex, it generally backfires and sex becomes more exploited and abused. Sex sells, whether it is in fashion, sports, television, movies, video, or politics. Look at the way people dress: trends are more sexy and revealing than ever, especially with women and young girls.

There are many contradictions in our society. Women want to feel safe in their boundaries with men, but also work hard to get their attention with sexuality. It is very complex. Consider the following questions and the motivations around the way you dress:

- What is your true motivation to dressing sexy?

- Is it to get attention?

- To get sexual attention?

- To feel good about yourself?

- To feel desirable?

- To express sexuality?

Advertising, television, and the movies are three of our biggest media empires and they are largely built around selling sex. Are you affected by the sexual messages in the content of the media? Consider how you are influenced by this as you answer the following questions:

- When do you participate in sexual games with people?

- When do you participate in sexual games with strangers?

- In times of increasing energy and awareness, do these games distract you?

- Do you connect with strangers on the freeway or in the subway, letting them into your energy field?

- Are you inviting predators in?

- How sacred is your energy to you?

- How sacred is the purity of the life force current that flows through you?

- Can you improve your sexual boundaries and have more clarity about the way you are understood sexually?

SEX AND RELATIONSHIPS

How many times have you been available for a connection with someone in your mind, or psychically with your energy? Try to examine what kind of energy you express and respond to all of the time. What you are open to?

What are you looking for when you connect with people? Is it to feel a rush of sexual energy? To flirt? To feel desirable? Does that excite you? I am not saying this is wrong—it depends on the intent. People can connect this way with respect and see each other's beauty and sexuality and choose to raise the connection to a higher place like the heart, or simply keep respectful boundaries. Sexual energy is an inherent part of the life force that allows us to propagate as a species. We learn to take responsibility for that energy.

The point of this section is to get you to think about where you stand. What is the right amount of sex and sexuality. Do other countries such as France and Brazil have healthier views about sexuality? Will more openness with sexuality create more or fewer problems? It is important for all of us to think about where we stand around these issues.

Overall, we must be more responsible around sexuality and clear about boundaries and intentions. It is increasingly important for me to deal in this area with the utmost integrity and purity. Any hooks or confusion in any of these areas can slow down the work and clarity around it. I am the one who enforces the rules and stays clear with myself.

Pornography

Pornographers have the right to free speech, and the First Amendment has protected their rights. Repression of sexual energy creates a need to live through sexual fantasy. Of course, there are many types of pornography and many enjoy the liberties it affords them. For some people, this is how they express themselves sexually; consequently, it is no surprise that pornography is one of the most lucrative businesses in the world.

I do not feel the need to judge porn, it is part of today's world. Most of us have computers and delete unsolicited porn from our e-mail inbox daily; however, I am opposed to any pornography that exploits the innocent or harms a person, such as pedophilia or the subjugation of women. The sexual predators who traffic in these underground activities should be accountable for their actions.

Sexuality is a powerful force. We benefit from clarity when it comes to rights and boundaries as sexual beings. All of us are created equal and are entitled to safety and choice of sexual preference and expression as long as it is not harming or taking energy from anyone else.

SECOND CHAKRA

Sexuality is the strongest component of the second chakra. The following five components lie in the second chakra:

+ Sexuality

+ Emotions

+ Money

+ Food

+ Creativity

These components are interconnected, much like a spiderweb; they feed into and out of each other. While the order of the components is different for each person, sexuality is the driving force that pushes all of the other components. As far as power and degree of importance, sexuality is at the top of the list. It is an area full of primitive survival instincts. Innate and strong, it is the driving force that propagates this planet.

Sexuality will continue to be discussed the most in this chapter because it is integral to the formula for healing of the second chakra. As discussed throughout the last section and this section, sexuality is the most important key for overall healing of the second chakra in individuals and the world.

Emotions are important components to your communication, expression, health, and healing. While they are a lesser component, they play an important role in healing the second chakra, and really are a means to an end for healing this area.

Although money is another important component to your comfort and lifestyle, it does not bring you peace and joy.

Rather, money affords you the luxury to experience certain elements and connection to "the love of power" within the second chakra. Money is powerful because it has the ability to affect other components such as the emotions and creativity. However, money is still more of a means to an end for healing the second chakra.

Food is a component that is less important yet closely tied into sexuality within the second chakra. Many times when sexuality is suppressed and the second chakra is out of balance, people turn to food by overeating, or they turn away from food with anorexia or bulimia. Food issues are another second chakra problem.

Creativity is the last component, which is very much a function of the balance or lack of balance within the second chakra. Sexuality, emotions, money, and food can all have some effect on creativity. When the second chakra is in balance, creativity abounds.

My Sexuality

To manifest sexual healing and freedom, I want to talk about my own sexuality. Much of my life I have felt controlled and unsatisfied with myself sexually. Growing up on a farm exposed me to the driving force of reproduction at a young age, and it infiltrated my bones. At the age of six, I had a sexual encounter with an older male cousin. We were playing the "doctor game," only as farm animals. I ended up being the mother cow and he wanted to suckle. Nothing much happened except me laughing and peeing in his mouth. Talk about surrealism! On a farm, a pulse of sexuality beats constantly and I got swept into sex at an early age.

That early imprint led to more sexual exploration. I felt my sexuality all the time. Masturbation became a part of my life around thirteen. I remember an awkward conversation with my dad as he explained that older boys showed him how to masturbate when he was young, that it was a sin, and I should not do it. Of course this piqued my curiosity, so I did it more, even though the Catholic guilt was firmly planted. The urge got stronger, the guilt got stronger and suppressed the power, the opening, and the beauty of my sexual expression. I learned not to trust the opening that came with an orgasm because of the idea that it was a sin, so the creativity of my second chakra was nipped in the bud and denied full expression. Also, my emotions were held back and controlled—God forbid that I should become an open, expressive, orgasmic man.

I have healed over the years and have enjoyed a nice expression of my sexuality in certain relationships, yet it is a fragile connection that is dependent upon free, open communication. I know there is room for more second chakra healing for me as there is with most people. To achieve this healing I need to be open and able to give and receive love; then, the sexual energy just seems to flow in a natural way.

The second chakra is the generator of "the love of power." I waste a lot of energy in this chakra. I know this is happening when I feel frustrated, lacking in power, stuck, sexually controlled, or even asexual. There is a better use for my energy, and better expression of my creativity. I know it and I am determined to uncover a deeper healing for myself. I am not looking for someone to come and heal me. I know the answers lie within my connection to God.

The "voice" is telling me I must slow down, connect to the earth, and let go of all things that are stressful and anxiety filled, so I can find the Spiritual flow of God moving directly through me. By feeling the Spirit, I am honoring the Spirit. The answers lie within the invitation for Spirit to reside within me. Everything I do is led by the Spirit of God; nothing is to be done because "I have to."

Within the act of love, Spirit now leads my flow of sexual energy. In my being, I have no room for any uses of sexuality that try to distract, capture, and control my Spirit. I have called forth the light for enlightened sexual expression, paving the way to trust my ability to give and receive love. As I find my way to this healing, I am confident that this Light can be shared with others.

HEALING MY UNIVERSE, HEALING THE PLANET

Light and awareness being brought to others cannot help but heal my universe. You may ask, "How can the planet heal? What can I do?" We could safely say, "Peace through understanding (head) and love (heart)." Yet, if there is so much confusion in the head and turmoil in the heart, we have to start lower, in the second chakra, where "the love of power" originates. We must find the way to clear the second chakra and work upward. It is my purpose to find my way through these obstacles within myself, within others, and within the greater collective of people on the planet. For this to be successful, I work upward from my second chakra. I am aware of the limitations I feel by being out of balance in my second chakra. My prescription for healing the planet begins with the following steps:

- I publicly acknowledge that I am healing my second chakra—I am not afraid to declare this.

- Being aware of any fears, feelings of being "less than," negativities, entitlements, past abuses, memories, doubts, impotencies, abuses, and abusings—I shed light on them all. I am now going through a passage with myself.

- Focusing on and learning every detail about my second chakra:

- Sexuality: anything unclear, any confusion, guilt or shame

- Emotions: holding, hiding, or protecting them

- Money: fears and concerns about lack

- Food: usage and comforts, mainly sugar

- Creativity: not trusting it, not using it, or destructing instead of constructing

When I get brutally honest with myself about sex, I realize that this has been an unfulfilled area and a suppressed and under-expressed chakra. I am attracted to women and I am heterosexual, even though I have had a couple of sexual encounters with men, which were more fulfilling as fantasies than as the actual experiences.

A definite strain of feminine energy runs through the men in my family. We are not closet homosexuals, yet feminine energy has generated some confusion on how to express it from time to time. For me, the healing work has been the strongest alignment and use of this energy, with acting running a close second. This feminine energy has a tremendous sensitivity to it and has been a great strength and asset to my masculinity once I learned to embrace it. It runs through all of my charkas, but has the strongest origins in my second chakra through my creativity and emotions. Ultimately, the feminine energy most resonates with my heart chakra, and that is why the second chakra must be clear: so that I can raise the feminine energy up to the heart. The heart chakra holds the key to love and healing and it is the true place for the feminine vibration.

EXPLORING THE SECOND CHAKRA

Although I have made peace with feminine energy, I believe it is in my lineage for a reason. My dad mentioned a couple of times that gay men approached him sexually when he was younger. The same thing has happened to me during my life. Were these experiences drawn to us to confuse us, to wake us up, to make us mad, or to give us a choice?

I believe that feminine energy exists on a soul level in our family's DNA, magnetizing experiences to move us along on our karmic paths, teaching us who we are. There are no victims in this world; on some level there is always choice and agreement. While it may be so far out of the conscious reality that it appears random and accidental, I believe my soul has known exactly what it was getting into.

I need to do more exploration to clear any remaining repression in my second chakra and to understand what is stuck there karmically. The list below contains the scenarios that I feel have karmic implications within my second chakra. Some of them may be past life memories that linger in my space to teach me something, to remind me who I am, and to possibly remind me where I came from. Some of them are future-oriented pictures and ones I have seen more recently. The pictures include:

- Creating a perfect match with a mature, happy, satisfied woman who loves being a wife

- Being a good dad to three or four children

- Reuniting with my ex-wife

- Not reuniting with my ex-wife

- Being asexual or non-sexual and lifting the energy up to the higher chakras, especially the throat and higher

- Having a polygamous relationship with many women and possibly having children with several of them

- Being a black slave and having sex with a white woman for no other purpose than pure sexual gratification

These are different scenarios that I believe have some karmic weight for who and what I am sexually. The top four are based more on a future reality, with some practical possibilities. The last three are based more on past lives, yet that does not mean they have no karmic reality or significance, even though the last two have very little. I am setting an intention to release the karmic pulls from these pictures and any other images affecting me. My goal is to clear these scenarios and their magnetizing power out of my space. While some of the images are more realistic than others, all of the scenarios have seemed real to me at one time or another, if only as dreams or flirting fantasies. Now, I prefer to choose my second chakra experiences, instead of being seduced or pulled into something by an unseen force, by coincidence, or even a future or past life concern.

I do believe I will create a relationship with a happy and mature female who loves being a wife, and I can definitely see myself being a dad to two more children. These are the pictures I am most intentional about and the most attached to. However, I have enough faith to give it all to God, and I do.

If your thoughts around sex are complicated, twisted, kinky, confused, shut down, child-like, or resentful, they can become cleaner, easier, and freer. If indeed it is part of my life purpose to create this formula to free the second chakra in people, then all of the steps we are going through in this chapter are important. I hope you are paying attention and thinking about all of this in yourself. I know this work can free you from confusion in the second chakra. The clearing will create room for choice. Conscious choice brings clarity, awareness, and healing to you. As we do this work with individuals, it will spread to the world.

What does your intuition tell you about your second chakra? Take an inventory of your second chakra. What is going on in there? What is your intuition saying to you about all of this? Do you need clearing in the second chakra?

SECOND CHAKRA CLEARING FORMULA

State your intention to clear your second chakra. This formula works better with a healer or someone who can guide you through the process. If you have no one to support you, proceed on your own and get help when you need it. Invoke your guides, teachers, and your higher self to lend assistance and witness this clearing. Get out your healing tools if you have any: sage, oils, or stones. Clear your work space. Cleanse yourself. Ask your guides to watch over you and support this healing.

+ Ground the base/first chakra into the earth. Visualize a taproot going down into the earth, at least 5 or 6 feet. The energy released and cleared will flow through the base chakra into the earth.

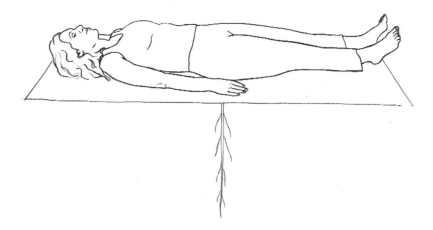

Figure 16a.

+ Start the breathing exercise and continue for 10 to 15 minutes. You want to feel your energy moving and body starting to tingle. Hold onto the stones.

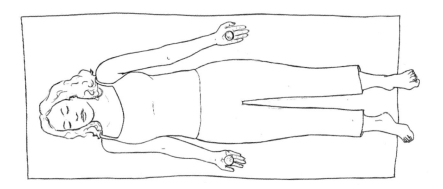

Figure 16b.

+ Connect to the base chakra; when it feels clear and grounded, move up to the second chakra.

- Focus your awareness on the second chakra. Use your imagination to describe what is in there.

- Is it open?

- Can you feel it spinning? If so, describe it in detail, and if not, then clear it.

- Clearing the second chakra: identify the blocks and break them down into these areas:

  Sexual
  Emotional
  Creative
  Money
  Food

- Bring awareness to each block.

- Exactly where is it located?

- What color, shape, temperature, and consistency is the energy?

- What does the stuck energy feel like?

- What does it say to you?

- Does it say it protects you?

- If the energy is not a pure color, such as a clear orange, know that it has negative energy in it and that takes energy from you. Connect to your higher self and replace it with a pure Light from your higher self. Where awareness goes, energy flows. Continue through each level. You will feel the blocks. Once they are cleared your whole body will vibrate; if it is not vibrating, resume the breathing.

- Is there a "love of power" in any of the five categories? Pay close attention to these areas. If there are feelings of arrogance and ego, it is an area that needs clearing. It may show up as an area that needs or wants some attention from the person helping you. Or if you are working alone, it will distract you and convince you to take a break or answer the phone.

When the second chakra is fully open and spinning, anchor this energy into the earth through the first chakra. Expand it upward to the heart chakra, gently allowing the energy to move through the third chakra (solar plexus). It should move through, but if it gets stuck, let go of the will. Let any battles of will melt away. The energy should easily move to the heart now. You are moving "the love of power" in the second chakra up to "the power of love" in the fourth chakra, or the heart.

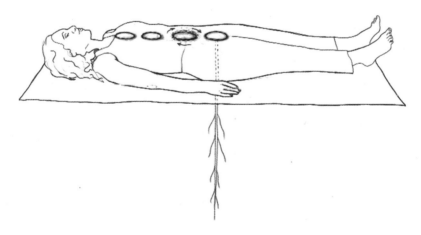

Figure 16c.

Bring your hands together in front of your heart as if you were going to pray, palms and fingers touching. Pull your hands apart one inch. Feel the energy moving between the fingers and hands. Pull the hands apart twelve inches, and slowly move them back together. Feel the energy, keep working with the energy, connect it from the heart to the hands. Now you are working with the energy of your heart. Feel the heat, vibration and love. It is powerful and very exciting to connect to the heart.

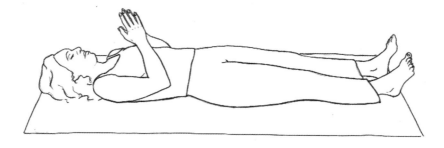

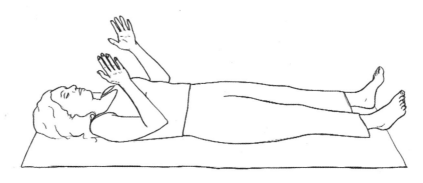

Figure 16d.

When this connection is strong, move your hands down over the second chakra. Continue with the same in and out motion of the hands, bringing them together as if in prayer, and apart again. Connect the energy into the second chakra. Balance it now. Work with it for a few minutes. Of course, where awareness goes, energy flows. Let the imagination be free to do its work here, then relax the hands on the pelvis over the ovaries or pelvic area. Just relax.

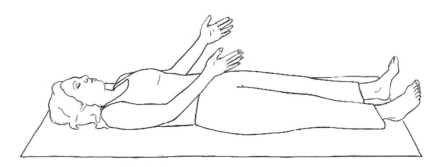

Figure 16e.

Feel the energy flowing from the heart through the right hand to the second chakra and back up through the left hand back to the heart. Feel the flow of energy between the two chakras. Continue to ground yourself into Mother Earth.

State the following: "My second chakra is clear. My heart is open to the power of love."

Thank your guides, teachers, and anyone who helped support you. Acknowledge yourself.

Work with your second chakra energy daily. Keep bringing it up to the heart. Practice keeping it clear and continue to affirm that it is clear. Record the changes in a journal to keep track of your progress. Expect your life to change dramatically and expect to realize your potential. The heart is an amazing navigation center. You are home. The second chakra can release all of its power to be used in the creation of the life you want to lead. Eventually the heart releases the second chakra energy to the throat for full expression, to the third eye for vision, and to the crown for connecting all there is. It is a powerful healing.

~c~

GROWTH, EXPANSION, POINT OF VIEW

In this chapter, I reveal my feelings about being an accomplished healer and master: my intuitive feelings about where this accomplishment is going to take me—possibly toward a role as a universal interpreter—and some basic conclusions about human evolution in terms of being a man. I conclude with the creative process and what writing this book has done for me.

This section represents the application to my life of all the material offered in this book. I do this to show you ways to tie the information together, so that you can do an overview of your life and subject matters that are important to you.

A MASTER

What does it take to allow yourself to be a master? Is it confidence? Ownership? Knowledge? Experience? When people give you the title of "master," does that make you a master?

I deal with the idea that I am a master. This would have been impossible for me to consider during my reluctant phase, and it is still not easy; yet, there is a shift happening now. I feel mastery downloading into my belief system, a mastery of getting out of the way and letting energy flow through me.

The accomplishment I feel as a healer has come from the experience of working with several thousand people over the years. I am confident because God has never let me down. The presence of a higher power always shows up for the healings.

A gathering of information takes place when I do the work. It is more about being open and holding the space for healing than it is about knowledge in my head. Much of the knowledge I have attained is about myself, and how to stay out of my own way, allowing God to do the work. As that process has taken place I am aware that my clarity as a healer has improved.

A witness to the truth, I feel good in the mastery of being a witness to the power of Spirit. When I hear the "voice" it is accompanied by Spirit and the combination of these two reveals a truth to me about myself, others, and life. I am a sensitive man, with a lot of intuition. There are many ways God gets my attention. The strongest way is when I hear the "voice." The "voice" has given me some degree of mastery as a healer. This mastery can be like a secret chamber. It can appear as if the master holds a special key, as if he or she knows something you do not. However, mastery is about simplicity and truth, which contribute to living life.

Mastery of life is not about the serious stuff, the struggle, the pain or the horror. Mastery of life is about freedom, love, joy and creativity. Mastery of life is about living. That is what is in the secret chamber. Mastery in the sense of healing is about all of these things. Healing and truly living life contain the same ingredients.

In my mid-forties, not a boy or a young man anymore, I am now middle-aged. Many of my life experiences were based on my waiting to live. In recent years, as the universe dictated that I become a healer, I became more aligned with being in the moment and giving God the space to be in my life. As a result, I found my way to more and more truth.

Is this true mastery? My humanity says no. Although I am an average person, information comes to and through me, information that is full of guidance, light, truth, magic, and mastery. I am willing to own that now, willing to step to the front of the line and say yes to the truth. I am willing to be a conduit for God to speak the truth without the hesitation of my past, without the fear of being judged or criticized. When you allow yourself to be a master of your own life, none of that matters.

I have embraced tremendous change in my life, with lessons that were formidable and that have increased my faith to practice what I preach. As I do this more and more, I find my acceptance around mastery is easier. When I just take the action to do the work, staying clear and using the healing tools, I find things work smoothly in my life.

UNIVERSAL INTERPRETER

What does the world need these days? World peace? The world needs leaders who speak a common language: the language of the heart. Universal interpreters—such as Martin Luther King, Jr., Gandhi, Mother Theresa, Nelson Mandela, Jimmy Carter, and Oprah Winfrey to name a few—can communicate with everyone because they stand for love and peace. They have the ability to rise above discord to further a higher cause.

Although I do not put myself in the category of those particular people, I feel I have a role in the world situation as a universal interpreter. I have offered my life to God, to show up and do the work.

A few years ago, I was in Brazil visiting some friends and doing some healing work. After spending most of my time in Rio de Janeiro, I decided to extend my trip to travel in the rain forest. I have always been drawn to the expanse and wildness of the forest and was excited to be adventuring there. A good friend, Rob, was traveling with me, also making his first trip into the jungle. It was a very quick trip (six days) enhanced by a specialized motorboat that got us into the interior of the forest. Nature was unbelievable and the people were even more amazing. This trip taught me the endless possibilities of communicating with others.

To further define what I mean by universal interpreter, in the Brazilian rain forest I encountered people who communicate with their third eyes. They communicate in pictures more than words, projecting pictures right into your consciousness. As I spoke no Portuguese, this was an effective way for them to communicate with me. I found it fascinating and used my third eye to express myself more than I ever had before. It was exciting to feel the third eye spinning, to send and receive pictures as a form of communication. The "voice" started telling me that I was a universal interpreter and that I should get comfortable communicating this way, and perfect this form of communication. I was very happy to learn that I could communicate this way and it proved to further expand my gift of Clairaudience into clairvoyance—clear seeing. The key was to use the gift. It was a unique foreign language to me. Even the children in the Amazon communicated this way. This form of sharing pictures and information was on a high psychic level. You learned there was little need to try and hide anything from these people, because they had already seen the pictures. I can see how this culture leads a simple, straightforward life, open and available for all to see.

Soon after coming home from Brazil, I read an article in the *Los Angeles Times* about Islamic fighters, many belonging to the Al Qaeda network, who were traveling around the world fighting their so called "holy wars." In this article, a villager in Chechnya said that dark foreigners moved into their village one night. They did not speak the local language, yet the foreigners had an amazing way of communicating what they wanted. "They sent pictures to your brain," he said. "It was eerie how these men moved like the wind." They were chameleon-like, blending in with the environment, yet they had actually come to Chechnya to cause fear and terror through violence and loss of life. In fact, they were seeking to create an Islamic state; in 2003, after several years of bombings and protests in Russia, Chechnya became a republic within the Russian Federation.

Beyond the violence and struggle for independence by the Chechnyan people and the added attention that the Islamic extremists brought to their scene, what interested me was a description about how these terrorists moved and communicated. They achieved a way of guerilla warfare that gave them abilities to move around places under the radar. They were able to communicate without language. The villager said you knew not to play games with these foreigners. Now, this is not to glamorize them or agree with their style of violence or their cause, but there is something for Americans to learn from all of this. Whether it is people from the rain forest or Muslim extremists, the world has some very advanced civilizations in it, even if they are behind the United States and other superpowers in wealth and technology.

I look at the world and I wonder where it is headed. The dynamics of good versus evil are firmly in place; however, deciding who is good and who is evil is tricky. Many of us are starting to doubt that we, the Americans, are the good guys, and it is difficult to comprehend the intention of our government. September 11 was tragic, and at first it certainly gave our government a kind of mandate to change our approach to human rights. Ultimately, that change created unpopular sentiment towards Americans throughout the world, and thus, the need for more universal interpreters working to bring healing to the world.

PERU

Have you ever had the feeling that you were being called into the middle of something? I first felt it in May 2001 at Machu Picchu in Peru, while traveling as a healer with a group of people. I was there because the "voice" had been bugging me to go to Machu Picchu for years. I arranged to spend some time at night on the grounds of the ruins. It was amazing. The "voice" would not be quiet; it said that I was to go to the Great Pyramid of Giza in Egypt and spend some time (possibly the night) in the king's chamber where information would be passed to me. I heard that the information would lead me to Mount Sinai, the Jordan River, and finally to the Dead Sea. Steven, a friend from the group, told me to forget about it, that it was too dangerous. I dropped the subject, thinking he must be right.

Later in November 2002, when I was in the Brazilian rain forest, the "voice" told me again to go to Egypt and Israel as soon as possible; there was information waiting for me, and I should plan to go to the pyramids, Mount Sinai, Jerusalem, Jordan River, the Sea of Galilee, and the Dead Sea. This time I paid attention, and I realized I was being chastised by the "voice" for letting fear stop me from going before.

In October 2003, I traveled to Egypt and Israel. I experienced amazing things, including wonderful treatment by Muslims, Christians, and Jews. The time in the Great Pyramid was powerful and intense, although the information was not as dramatic as my ego wanted. I quickly let go and just let it be what it was. The main message was to find the joy among all people, get used to the crowds, and to prepare myself because many were coming.

I felt something shift in me during my time in the Middle East. It was as if I traveled endlessly back in time to an era of rocks, caves, camels, deserts, and donkeys. I am aware I have roots and lifetimes in the Middle East, and after being there a while, I realized I could be safe there and that I would return one day soon.

My Role

I believe my role as a universal interpreter is to help humanity wake up and remember who we are. In order to wake up, we must turn on the Light by awakening our energetic bodies. Once the Light is on in people and they are aware of it, universal interpreters will step forward as beacons and help guide others to their awakenings. The masses are ready to be led into the Light of greater consciousness, a conscious awareness that we are all one.

Humanity needs the freedom that the Light offers to disengage from the machine, the matrix, the system, the way that lives are controlled by fear. This Light contains individual freedom and the ability to raise personal consciousness to the heart, to the power of love. The power of love is a connection that is occurring through a web of Light bringing us all together. I have seen this connection: it looks like a spiderweb of light connecting us to each other and to all things. Like our energy, when we awaken to the web of Light, it is always there; it is just a matter of tuning into it.

I am concerned about the world situation; not afraid, but concerned about the changes coming our way. These changes on the issues of political, economical, environmental, and health will make the world a more uncertain place. In the healing work, I have noticed that humans do not embrace change and the unknown easily. We are creatures of habit, and we do not like change. The unknown drives fear into man's experience. However, connecting to Light as a source of illumination exposes and reduces fear. It gives you faith. "Keep focused on the Light" has been my mantra in times of change. Universal interpreters will know the power of love and Light.

Universal interpreters will move among cultures easily and possess abilities to heal, as well as, to communicate with all people. I foresee that interpreters will be brought forward to mediate between nations. I believe I was led to the Middle East, the Amazon, and Peru to come to an understanding of what is happening in the world, and as training sessions to experience the universality of love, and love's ability to communicate and heal through any kind of barrier.

Media is helping the world become one. In other ways, communication systems are creating more tension and disharmony. Negative forces, such as terrorism, use the media as free advertising for their intentions to do harm to others. The result of the overload of media is a fear-based population that eventually becomes desensitized, needing a reality shock to feel anything. We hear about bombs and death and we tune them out; thus we lose our feelings and require bigger and bigger events, with bigger shock value, to get our attention. Therefore, we need more Light to bring harmony back to our sensitive souls. Can you play a role in healing a volatile world?

Although there are great pioneers out there pulling for peace, it would seem the world is moving farther from peaceful accord. Consequently, I feel compelled to use the term universal interpreter to describe healers doing the work of love through Light. We need an army of peaceful universal interpreters to bring about healing across the cultures of the world. You could be one of the universal interpreters waiting for the moment to remember who you are. Your time of awakening is near.

BEING A MAN

Allow me to pose a question on behalf of males everywhere: when can we ease up and enjoy living? This is not to exclude women, because whatever I say about men is a direct result of what women are doing, and vice versa. In this section, I look at how we are evolving as a species. It seems that men are becoming more feminine and women are becoming more masculine. Is this path of evolution affecting our abilities around fertility and conception? Are we creating problems with reproduction that may affect us in the future? In my recent work, there have been more people experiencing fertility problems. Many factors such as women being older as they give birth are contributors to the problem; however, I believe that sexual imbalances are hampering fertility.

Men's accepted role as the provider and the protector has changed over the years. Their sensitive, or feminine, sides are developing and becoming commonly accepted in today's society. Is there resistance from men about expectations of them? Do we need to hang on to some of our age-old masculine traits to continue to feel our manhood?

I have not resisted the New Age development of men, yet there are times when I do not want to be sensitive, times when I declare that I cannot be as sensitive as a woman may want me to be. These situations never go well; they create breakdowns in the flow of communication within relationships. So, why do they happen? It is okay to set boundaries around not communicating. It does not mean it is a permanent occurrence.

Being less than sensitive is okay. For the record, I am pro-communication and pro-relating; nonetheless, it is good to have a break every once in a while.

For instance, Billy and Karen, friends of mine, have a successful relationship. They have one night off a week where they go their separate ways. They may hang out with friends, be alone, or do something for themselves. They just do not have to show up in the relationship for anything specific. This freedom gives them the ability to detach and keep freshness in the relationship.

Does increased femininity in men cause a loss of sexuality? I feel that I lose something when I am always attuned to someone else's needs. Again, am I rebelling against the way a female partner wants me to be, or am I rebelling against becoming too feminine? I know that I am an extremely sensitive man. Sometimes I do not need to be so in tune and receptive, I want a break, to be left alone and allowed to return to the relationship when I am ready.

I need to express myself in the world at large, rather than be consumed in one primary relationship. This does not mean that I do not want to be in one primary relationship; it means that I am looking for more meaning and expression of myself.

I look at the Spiritual pulls of my soul, my need to create, express, do, and experience. How does this tie into being a man? I am trying to figure that out. I know I am here to do something, something bigger than being a healer, a husband or even a father. My manhood includes all of these things and more, and is still evolving.

When I say bigger, I am not referring to an egotistical gratification, but to an energy explosion like a jet plane engine firing up on the runway. I feel I have only been on the runway of my life so far, and am now ready for the flight. The information wants to come through, and the guidance is lining up to help in this process. I am talking about the full embodiment of myself as a man and as a being of Light. There is maleness and femaleness in this energy, and an urgency to do and to accomplish in the world; to make peace with this urgency. I let go and enjoy the ride.

In my many roles, I move along in my life as a man in a way that sometimes feels out of control; yet, I always have choice in what I want to experience. Being a man is a complex endeavor, as is being a woman. We cannot turn back the hands of time, and we will have to make the best of it. The timing of it all and the evolution of man and woman will make perfect sense one day.

Neither too sensitive nor too feminine, I feel the need to put my foot down and say that is all for now: give me a break; let me rest; let me prepare for the "many" that are coming. Maybe that is the real reason for this chapter.

CREATIVE PROCESS

Writing this book was healing for me. Using and expressing my creativity allowed me to grow up as a man and helped me in the clearing of my second chakra. I now believe in myself as never before. I had tremendous love and support while getting this book done, and managed to manifest just the right amount of fear and insecurity to keep me guessing. I learned that I can finish a creative venture, even my first attempt to write a book. I see that when I do not use my creativity, I get lethargic and have to work to get back in shape.

Most of all, I have experienced that God wants to work through me many different ways and that writing is just one way. Through the writing process, I realized that if you use your creativity to express your life purpose, you will heal. Living your life purpose may be an easier way to heal than actually focusing on the healing itself.

~~

CHAPTER TEN

HEALING AND WORLD EVENTS

Violence, September 11, and the Middle East are subjects I find myself constantly revisiting. Exploring these challenging areas provides us with the opportunity to heal as individuals and as a society. My intention in this chapter is to stimulate your point of view to enable you to discover further clarity and to use your senses to recognize what rings true for you regarding world events. My hope is that new clarity will allow you to travel in new directions to receive the healing you seek. Where awareness goes, energy flows.

VIOLENCE

I do not condone or accept violence in any form; however, few places in the world are spared its repercussions. As humanity supposedly evolves, you might think we would become a more peaceful planet. The opposite seems true as the methods of warfare become more powerful and the violence and threat of violence becomes more extreme.

Violence is a problem of the second chakra, stimulated and controlled by "the love of power," which is a universal problem prevalent throughout the world. It translates from being an external problem in the world to an individual problem within most of us. When you live in fear, you are susceptible to abuse from a predator-like energy that seeks to control you. Fear creates the platform from which control can take place. When people are collectively controlled by fear, there is a point when the suppression starts to break people down, incurring rebellion. They give up hope and take up desperate measures to be heard, and violence ensues. A predator may be an energy, person, group, company, or state that takes from others, or destroys others for gain. I refer to the predators as the dark forces or dark energies that control others though fear and pain or the threat of fear and pain.

How easy is it for you to turn the other cheek when innocents and loved ones are harmed? It is not easy to turn the other cheek when struck or abused. I believe in taking an energetic stand against the dark forces and the fear on which they thrive. I stand firm, anchored into the Light, with my feet on the ground, and with the palm of my right hand facing the dark energy. I use my hand to stop the energy flow, and by saying, "No!" or "Stop!" to the dark energy, I establish an energetic boundary to this energy. This provides a shielding affect from the violent energy, which is based in fear and control. I have seen this action stop the dark energy in its tracks. Again, this is where awareness comes into the picture. You take control of your world when you take an active stand for what is right within you. Light, illumination, freedom, peace, love, free will, harmony, respect, openness, and faith all promote a state of calmness within. When peace is present, there is little need for expression through violence.

> John, a forty-two-year-old architect, had always had an intense relationship with his partner, Rick. John knew Rick to be brilliant in his work, though suffered from severe bouts of depression. When Rick was in a bad way, John avoided him, knowing a negative situation would occur if they discussed the depression. John felt he might get attacked by Rick and

*his darkness, and end up feeling bad himself. He was even
beginning to think he had a depression problem, too. He was
preparing to leave the architecture firm when we started to
work together.*

*I showed John how to shield himself from the dark energy
Rick carried. We worked on areas where John was unconscious about the power he gave to his own fear. He was afraid
to take a stand for himself against these dark energies. These
areas of fear were what brought him together with Rick in the
first place. Their karma was to experience similar veins of
fear and darkness, even though Rick's was much stronger,
and to learn through each other. In our work, John learned
how to peacefully stand in the Light and continue to love
himself in the presence of Rick's depression. He put his hand
up to the dark energy a few times to let it know he would not
take it on or be controlled by it. Their relationship changed
dramatically when John stepped through his fear. As he set
his boundaries with the dark energy within himself, it helped
him confront it externally in his world. He is no longer afraid
of darkness. This has also helped Rick start to deal with his
depression, too, and their firm is doing better than ever.*

The one area in which we can control violence is within ourselves. When we are at peace within ourselves, as well as our
experiences with violence around us, we take on a different perspective. Freedom comes from realizing that you have a choice
in your experience with violence. Choice is enhanced by the
awareness that fear could be controlling you. Confusion is lifted
when you are able to see through the illusion created by the
dark forces.

Remember, fear is about the future, and its power is based on
the anticipation of being hurt. Pain is about the past, and its
power is based on a memory of being hurt at another time. The
combination of these energies separates you from the moment
where true power exists. When you are out of your power, it is
easy to be controlled or herded like sheep. People react out of

fear, anger, suppression, rage, control, and domination. This happens on all levels, individually and collectively.

As individuals we must understand violence, aggression, control, and domination, and avoid being controlled by them. We can learn from what is happening in the world and do our part to hold the space for peace. World peace starts at home, right here inside of you.

THE UNITED STATES AND THE WORLD

The United States is at war somewhere in the world most of the time. The war on terrorism exploded with the second Bush administration. If it was a holy war for Muslims, why were we dragged into the battle? We say the solution is democracy, whether it be in Afghanistan, Iraq, Israel, Iran, or simply the Middle East. The United States is stuck in a battle of the second chakra over "the love of power" with many countries around the world. Not just the Middle East. This is more than the need for worldwide democracy, it is about oil, money, nuclear energy, land, natural resources, religion, power, and control all playing a role in what the United States is doing in the world. It feels like there is confusion and a lack of integrity around many of these issues. And the confusion is creating opportunities for our ethics to be challenged.

How do terrorists divide, confuse, and intimidate a powerful nation like the United States? They are able to do this when there is doubt about the true motivation of our country's actions. This doubt lives within many Americans, as well as, people around the world. Terrorists have not conquered the United States, yet they have certainly affected every American's life in some way. They have our attention. They have a purpose about what they are doing.

As conflicts with Muslim nations continue to escalate, watch the polarities that will probably occur: Arab vs. Jew, United States vs. the world, Islam vs. Infidels, Fundamentalist Christian vs. Fundamentalist Muslim, American vs. Terrorist, Bush vs. Non-Bush.

The United States' stand as administrators of democracy affects our primal survival issues. Do you want to participate in the war or just watch it on TV? Do you feel rage towards terrorists like Bin Laden or Al Qaeda? Does their violence push you to violent feelings of revenge? Is it their plan to polarize Americans? Are they effectively bringing the war home to each of us as individuals? How much more anger will you feel if gas goes to $3 or $4 a gallon? What does it take to affect you? Events like September 11, terrorist plots, or the price of gasoline?

My Personal Violence

For clarity, I start at home and look at the violent forces within myself. I recognize a strain of violent male energy within myself that has on occasion been expressed. This is an energy in my DNA that gets stimulated along the way. The violence in me is not an active energy, yet it does arise when self-defense is needed. I have had physical fights with my father and other people, although I have never started a fight. The incidents began as acts of self-defense, yet there was violence in them. Punches were thrown, and once a gun was drawn on me. Compared to war, this is minor—or is it?

Warrior energy is warrior energy, innately. I do not see it as feminine. I think about the verbal and psychic battles I have had in my life. How aggressive did I allow my thoughts to be? How deep did I allow my comments to penetrate? How much damage and pain did I inflict? I realize this is the stuff of which wars are propagated. These are the basic training exercises that teach us aggression. Most of us know a lot about violence.

I am still learning to psychically set boundaries against the dark forces. Protection as a form of self-defense is not a dark energy, it is a way of dealing with dark energy. In other words, when you seal yourself off against violent dark forces, you save yourself a possible battle for "the love of power." When you illuminate the dark energies with Light and diffuse their power, you are transcending the control of the lower vibrations of fear and pain and taking them to a vibration of love.

THE POWER OF LOVE

Within my life's purpose as a healer, father, and writer, I am committed to being a non-violent person and to bring consciousness to my thoughts and my psychic intentions. My thoughts must be peaceful. I do not believe it is right to use force, power, intellect, or energy to overpower someone. I am here to lead, teach, and follow to the best of my human abilities through the "power of love." Peace can be created and experienced through our choice to vibrate the power of love through our hearts, and throughout the land. Do nice guys finish last? Perhaps, but then again, nice guys may not be participating in the race or battle; they may be focused on peace.

A housewife named Cheryl came to me seeking help for a violent temper. She was known to go into fits of rage and destroy breakable items by throwing them at her husband, the wall, or whatever was in front of her. When she came to me, all of her focus was on what was being done to her by others. Once we opened her perspective to include what she had the power to create, we started to get a handle on her anger. Cheryl had deep issues of violence to work through within herself. It was ugly at first and we had to clear some very dark energy that sought to possess her without her knowing about them. These energies were strong magnets for angry violent people and she had several of them in her life. As the dark energies were exposed and cleared, Cheryl became a different person. The rage slowly subsided, and her husband decided it was safe to come home again.

Power is surrounded by illusion, and those who are obsessed with power are generally lacking in faith. I am truly examining faith in my life. To strike out where fear is present through a lack of faith is an easy reaction. My faith comes from the way that I treat myself. When there is peace and harmony within me, there is no desire or need for violence. If I treat myself harshly, it is easier to fall into a pattern of self-abuse and self-violence; like the old saying, when you are treating yourself badly, you kick the neighbor's dog. This is how a lot of the violent behavior in our world occurs. People are negative and hard on themselves, so they take it out on others. When we point a finger at someone, we have three fingers pointing back at us. Here is the way I look at the contributing factors to violence and peace:

LOVE OF POWER → Fear → Suppression → Control → Anger → Rebellion → **Violence**

POWER OF LOVE → Faith → Openness → Freedom → Happiness → Harmony → **PEACE**

Figure 17. Love of Power

To be effective crusaders for peace, let us start with ourselves. Take care of the violence within yourself, then go forth into the world talking about peace. To confront the dark forces that perpetuate non-peaceful actions, let us stand in the Light to illuminate the fear on which the dark side depends. Universal interpreters operate from this place. I like the analogy of striking a match in a pitch-black cave. When the match is lit, the darkness is illuminated.

The slogan "Just say no!" is another great analogy. I believe in the power of the word "No." I believe it cuts the psychic cords or the power that is being exerted through negative, fear-based energy. Saying no brings conscious awareness and boundary to the moment in a forceful, clean, energetic way. When boundaries are clear, violence may be unnecessary. The dark energies usually turn away and look for easier targets: those who are afraid, unaware, or have unclear boundaries. Where awareness goes, energy flows, and "no" is the clearest, cleanest boundary I know.

SEPTEMBER 11, 2001

September 11 produced a tremendous amount of courtesy

and human respect in our country for about a month, then it slowly faded. The event forced people to face lifelong fears about mortality, pushing many into a frozen state of fear.

> *For instance, Susan, a high school student, was traumatized by September 11. She was afraid something was going to happen in Los Angeles, and it took days for her mom to get her out of the house. Once we worked and cleared some of the fear she took on, it became apparent her mom was just as afraid. I ended up having the mom come into the session and we worked on her, too. As they released the fear they carried, the energy lifted and they both left in good Spirits.*

On September 11, the planet was suddenly covered in a layer of molecular fear. We were all breathing it in. My instincts were to start cleansing my body on September 12, and I started exercising more to keep my pores open and help my body to continue releasing fear and negativity.

Since then, change has been rampant. The vibrations on the earth are speeding up with each full moon and with each physical shift or change on the earth. Our country will recover; however, reminders of that day will be etched into our memories forever.

Some people seized the opportunity to get honest with themselves and to make changes in their lives. They quit their jobs because they were not happy. Others did the opposite, holding on to the past for dear life, unwilling to change with the times.

> *Louis, a mortgage broker, was unhappy with his life. He expressed desires about quitting his job before September 11; afterwards, he was so afraid, that he denied having ever expressed an interest in quitting. He said he needed to hold onto his job now, as he may not be able to get another. Any faith he had before the disaster quickly vanished.*

During the next several months, I saw many people freeze up with fear. Many returned to old relationships, as this event made people afraid to be alone. Another client, Nancy, told me that the first thing she did was call her ex-husband. They decided to get back together that day. Unfortunately, it proved to be a rash decision and they split up again after three weeks, realizing the safety of each other was not the solution to their fears. This was not an uncommon occurrence during this time.

I found it important to listen to my guides at this time and to take action around my dreams; henceforth, the writing of this book. For me it was about moving forward: to not buy into the fear and to invest in my faith.

September 11 gave me more faith about being on the right path. And, I saw a greater need for healers to be on the frontier leading people through the darkness to the Light. I believe September 11 was a wake-up call for modern day messengers of the world. The time to make a difference is now.

MIDDLE EAST

In the past, I felt apathy, bigotry, and ignorance about the Middle East, and I was tired of hearing about Israel, Palestine, Afghanistan, Iraq, suicide bombings, and terrorism. We cannot afford to be an apathetic nation anymore, yet do we know the truth? How do we find it out? Can the truth be found within ourselves about a place as far away as the Middle East?

So the question arises, "What is the United States' role in world politics?" Do you care? Are you personally in alignment with American policy towards our foreign brothers and sisters? Maybe it is time to learn more about the world situation and take a stand for the kind of world you want to live in. What else can you do? Can you be a peaceful warrior, or a universal interpreter during this violent time? Someone emitting peace and harmony, bringing solace to your family, school, or neighborhood? Where do you stand regarding the Middle East in your life?

While drama in the Middle East creates unrest, fear, and anxiety, it could also prompt spontaneous healing or personal meltdowns, depending on your approach. Explore Middle East issues to discover your truth about them, aside from what you hear on the news. Make a choice about what it will teach you. Will you learn about fear, faith, violence or apathy? Take it to a personal level, seek the lesson, find the healing for yourself, then you can make a difference in the world.

TRIP TO THE MIDDLE EAST

My trip to Egypt and Israel was meant for gathering information about the area and to satisfy a persistent calling from the "voice" to travel there. It became so strong that I realized I would have to go or else not find any peace in my waking time. I was being told to go to the pyramids in Giza, Mount Sinai, Jerusalem, the Dead Sea, Qumran, the Jordan River, and the Sea of Galilee. I was able to visit them all, with many stops in between. And, I must report, I met wonderful people along the way. I spent equal time with Christians, Jews, and Palestinians. I was treated equally well by them all. We are all the same: people are people. Some good, some impatient, some happy, some sad; we are all the same.

Upon my return, people asked me if I found what I was looking for. I told them I did not know what I was looking for. I went because I was compelled to go. I do not know all of the reasons yet, but I know God has a plan for me. I was sent on many interesting excursions and I felt as safe as in downtown Los Angeles, maybe even safer. It was not about being afraid, nor about being stupid. I was cautious and aware and had a few moments of dealing with people who are starving and trying to make a living. It does not take long once you leave the United States to realize just how good we truly have it in this country. I marvel at the things we take for granted and I always feel good passing through customs to be greeted by a welcome home.

~~

CHAPTER ELEVEN

MIRRORS

Everything that happens to you is a mirror in which to see yourself. What you see depends on what you set yourself up to experience. When you are conscious and set intentions about what you choose to experience, life can be a breeze.

In the prior chapter we looked at the world situation, which is a huge external mirror. In this chapter we look closer to home. We look at relationships, couples work, family, and divorce. My intention is to bring clarity to these areas, to the mirrors they provide, and to the lessons they teach.

RELATIONSHIPS: COUPLES

All external relationships mirror our relationship with ourselves. I believe the people we choose to relate to represent something about ourselves. This is a positive thing and growth comes from it.

For relationships to endure, there must be growth, change, and evolution. If people are willing and committed to working on a relationship, it will grow and prosper. We cannot expect relationships to stay the same, as nothing in nature does. Where there is growth, it may not all be positive; some things may appear negative.

For instance, Danny and Paula, a married couple in their thirties, had spent fifteen years together. They hit a difficult spot when Paula confided she had been having an affair; apparently she was not getting her communication needs met with Danny. He took her for granted and Dexter, her affair partner, was great at communication. They had fun together and could talk for hours. Paula admitted she was mad at Danny, although she did not want to hurt him. She was not ready for a divorce; nevertheless, there needed to be some changes for her to stay. Danny got the message, and after he recovered from his damaged ego, he realized he did not want a divorce either. They worked it out and reconnected in a better way. Paula was able to let go of Dexter and get the communication she needed from Danny. Some couples cannot recover from the negativity created from an affair. Danny was able to see that Paula was trying to get his attention, and he forgave her without needing to punish her. Neither of them wanted a divorce and they were able to work out their differences and reaffirm their commitment to each other.

What we choose to do with the negative tests our commitment to the relationship. When people are committed to working on a relationship, it will grow stronger through adversity. Then, the good times are more meaningful and there is a stronger platform to change and evolve.

Danny and Paula came through this test together in a stronger way than before. They realized there were places they felt stunted because most of their adult experiences were with each other. Their mirrors of the world were reflected most in each other. While experimenting with the affair, Paula realized she had power to get her needs met. She realized she was not crazy for wanting more communication from Danny, and that there were men who would love to communicate with her. If she could get it from Danny, she did not need to get it elsewhere.

Danny realized he was taking Paula for granted. He put his work, his friends, and his golf game before her. Making it through this test took them to the next level in their relationship. They realized they had been procrastinating about having children. When Paula mentioned it several times to Danny, he always said he was not ready. Through this deepening of the relationship and recommitting, Danny proclaimed that he was ready for children. Paula was ecstatic and began to understand that the problems and turmoil of the affair created the space for their relationship to grow.

Let us not get too heady, New Age, or idealistic about relationships, because we need to live our lives. Sometimes, you are at a place where you must make choices about where you want your relationship to go. With choice comes responsibility. The choice to work on a relationship with a partner gives you the foundation for an enduring relationship. And, your ability to demonstrate your choices will breed confidence.

Relationships break down when one or both parties cease the work of building, changing, and growing the relationship. They withhold their participation. They stop taking responsibility for where they want the relationship to go. Ultimately, the relationship stops growing. Relationships can endure this for a period of time, depending upon the strength of the foundation.

Everyone hits plateaus when they need downtime, yet it is important to be aware of those times and communicate them to our partners. And, it is important to shift out of these periods without becoming lazy or stuck.

Cindy and Mark were a young couple with two young children, ages two and four. Cindy was a full-time housewife and Mark worked to support the household. Mark had a good job, but he complained that the kids got all of Cindy's energy. Cindy said, "If you want me to have something left for you, I need some downtime." Mark thought she said, "I need some damn time!" So he agreed to hire a nanny. Cindy started to work out and take time away from the children for the first time in four years. She even took a weekend trip away with some girlfriends to Las Vegas. She got her downtime and eventually Mark got his wife back.

Women are generally the seekers when it comes to growth and change, and men are generally content not to rock the boat. As seekers, women want deep, meaningful communication. Often, they find it necessary to go outside the relationship to get what they seek. Although this can result in intimate connections outside the primary relationship, it does not necessarily translate to infidelity. Women need to talk, express themselves and be heard, and to get a response. Men are not always interested in deep personal communication; on a gorgeous, sunny day, they may want to be outside, clean the garage, or play basketball with their buddies. This is when laziness and bad habits about communication can get started.

A woman may get tired of nagging about couples' time together, and a man may resent these expectations and her disappointment about disconnection. This is where the commitment to work on the relationship is key. Both partners must invest themselves in pulling the relationship out of the doldrums; it cannot always be the responsibility of one person. In successful relationships, there is willingness from both sides to take responsibility. Occasionally, the non-communicator in the couple can say, "We need to talk. What's going on here?" And, this person might pay a few compliments on a regular basis, instead of just on birthdays and holidays.

In Danny and Paula's case, Danny learned he needed to ask Paula, "How was your day, honey?" even if he knew she stayed at home and had an easy day. It was the effort to communicate that Paula appreciated. After that, she was much more approachable for a kiss or some intimacy. Danny learned about how communication was Paula's foreplay. If he hoped to play, he better get some communication in the forefront.

Do men come from Mars and women from Venus? How do people take great information, great ideas, and make them work in their relationships? There are no guarantees; nevertheless, the one prerequisite I look for is a commitment to work on the relationship. If the commitment is there, a relationship can make it through anything. And if the parties involved take a step back and see the mirror that the other person is providing, they can have an experience together that is truly blessed.

> *To end this section with Danny and Paula, you may not be surprised to know that they now have a child and are very happy together. They have both moved out of comfort zones and habits within themselves and in the relationship together. Their love for each other far outweighs the need to end the relationship. In choosing to stay together, work through adversity and grow, they now have a wonderful marriage. They were always perceived as an ideal couple because of their long-term marriage, and through their commitment to work things out, Paula and Danny are still an ideal couple.*

DIVORCE

Life is full of interesting moves and maneuvers that are expected and unexpected. I have divorced, and in the process, I learned so much about life, letting go, change, judgment, fear, faith, and growth. It was difficult, and it pushed me to walk my talk. At one point, I turned to God and said, "I give it all to you, all the pain, the fear, and the hurt." I had faith at this moment, faith that grows now, every day. I saw the illusion of what I thought the relationship was supposed to be, and I have accepted the reality of what it was.

I made peace with the idea that our relationship was a success, not a failure. We have a beautiful child, Ruby, whom we both love dearly. The world is a different place because of our daughter. I am there for her as a parent just as I was when I was with her mom. This allows me to be friends with my ex-wife, to hold space for her growth and happiness and to form a bond that is comfortable for the development of our daughter.

Divorce is a powerful teacher that can move you forward to confront your future. I had to deal with my own happiness and I am happier now than I was. With no blame towards my ex-wife or myself, it was simply necessary to step aside and disengage from what was not working in our relationship. Neither of us was willing to continue to work on the relationship that we had established. The healthiest result seemed to be a parting of ways.

I dealt with a fair amount of self-criticism about how this would appear to my past, present, and future healing clients. I learned that although it was an issue for some, it was more of an issue for me. Once I made my own peace with the divorce, it was okay for everyone involved. The peace in me outweighed any external negativity that may have been trying to get my attention. A part of me that had to let go of the "happily ever after" dream and the belief that I had to be the role model for the perfect family. I realized that as a couple, we were a mirror for many people about their relationships.

I am an advocate of marriage and long-term, committed relationships between two well-suited people who co-create a system of life that works. That is a lifestyle that is hard to beat. I also admit that divorce is a possible solution when a marriage is not a good fit.

I have a number of friends and clients who I see demonstrating a lifestyle together that works. In Paula and Danny's case they were able to evolve together after one glitch. They realized they were best suited to stay in a long-term relationship with each other. There is little doubt they are over the hurdle now and know where they are going together.

A gay couple, Ben and Alex, have been together for a decade. They have each sacrificed comfort and routine in their lives and careers to accommodate the other's wishes and dreams. They bicker and tease back and forth, yet it is never in a way that makes friends uncomfortable to be around. Their relationship is on very solid ground and they have made a commitment to be together for life. You breathe in a sense of stability when you are around them. You feel good.

ORPHANS AND ADOPTED PEOPLE

At least once a month I see a new client who was adopted. In almost every case, the clients are women in their thirties, most at a point in their lives when they feel anxiety and angst and are having trouble with their relationships. This is usually what drives them to me. When I find out they are adopted, I know it is time for them to find their biological family. The need to connect with biological parents arises in a powerful way, and in every instance thus far, the client has been able to find her birth parent or parents within a few weeks, if they are still alive. More than once, the child arrived as the parent was on their deathbed, offering a last opportunity to resolve the relationship. It is not a coincidence that Spirit drives these reunions.

Susan, a thirty-nine-year-old painter, came to see me with an issue about getting pregnant. It just was not happening. The "voice" told me to ask her about her father. She said she was adopted and did not know her biological parents. I told her I thought it was important for her to learn about her father and possibly meet him. Wondering how it would help, she agreed to start the search. After contacting the adoption agency, she learned her biological mother had recently contacted the agency asking about her, and she had left updated information about being contacted. Susan followed up and met her mom and heard her story for the first time. They bonded with amazing ease. She learned her mom was fifteen when she got pregnant, and her family sent her away to have the baby and give it up for adoption right away. Although Susan knew some of the factual story, it was not as real until she heard it for herself. Her mom said she recently felt the need to meet her daughter. Susan asked about her father and learned her mom knew he lived in a nearby town. He was a painter. She followed the lead and found her father and met with him, as he was on his deathbed with cancer.

Susan had many epiphanies after meeting her parents, but nothing like seeing her dad's paintings. It was more than eerie, for their work was very similar. Suddenly Susan learned where she came from. She started to understand why she felt the way she did about things. Her father died a short time after meeting her, and they completed what they needed to together. This situation was a lengthy healing process for Susan, and she has recently succeeded in getting pregnant. We are all quite sure that the healing helped her clear some energies that were in the way of her getting pregnant. Somewhere, there had been a feeling that she was not worthy of love and a child. She believed she would fail at the responsibility of parenthood.

Adopted women often experience difficulty getting pregnant. My intuition tells me that they need this completion about where they came from before they can bring a child into the world. Likewise, it seems the birth parent may need this completion before they can move on in their journey. I am sure this is not always the case; but nevertheless, adopted people coming to me for healing have consistently shown me these indications.

Another interesting trend with adoptees is a tendency for past or present drug and/or alcohol abuse. I believe this is a result of deep-seated fears about being unlovable and fears of trusting. This starts at birth when the baby is passed from the biological parent, who is often immersed in guilt and shame, to a nurse, adoptive parent, or agency representative. The child feels negative energy and takes it into his or her body. Later, the adoptee may have the feeling that there is something wrong with him or her, and that he or she is not loveable, quite possibly resulting from the negative energy acquired a long time ago.

The best way to bring healing to an adoptee is to unravel this at the source; that is, to tell the client to contact their biological parent, to discover who they are and where they came from. Parents may have a set of stories ready about why they did what they did, and it may not be a pretty reunion. The child is fast to assess the situation (e.g., I have her eyes, he was an alcoholic, she was an artist) and to glean what is needed from the parent or parents.

It is most important for the adopted child to come in contact with his or her mother. After all, the child had a nine-month relationship with her, and the mother usually has most of the information the child seeks. She probably has information on the father, too. Often, the father is no longer connected to the mother, which may be the reason why the child was given for adoption.

Karen, at thirty-four, came to me with relationship problems. I knew she was adopted. The "voice" said, "She needs to meet her mom." Karen fought me on it but went ahead and located her mom's contact information. She refused to believe her relationship insecurities could come from being adopted, for she had good adoptive parents. I told her about the guilt being passed when she was handed over. She said, "How could I remember that? I was only a few days old." I told her the cells remember it, the feeling passes into the subconscious and lodges there. She understood that and eventually called her mom. Her mother sent her a picture and talked with her at length on the phone. The mom could not meet with her because her family did not know about Karen. They planned to meet one day. The connection with her mom, albeit by phone and photo, really helped Karen. I feel certain they will meet one day, and I know it has helped Karen already.

From a human behavior or human characteristic perspective, we hunger for our roots. When we don't know where we are from, or have not been told the truth about who we are, we know it and feel it deep inside. To have this intuition validated is an opportunity for a huge healing; it is like returning home.

For adopted people, healing is not dependent upon creating a fulfilling relationship with a biological family, it is about the connection to who they are.

When my clients feel the urge to find their biological family, the birth parents often feel it, too. There seems to be a cord pulling the parent and the child together at the same time. Parents tend to wait to take action due to guilt, yet they still feel the pull. Once either party expresses the desire for contact to an adoption agency, the agency will share the information if the other desires contact, too. The agencies seem to know when Spirit is calling for a reunion and a healing. Ultimately, we all need to know the truth about who and what we are; we need this to get to where we are going.

These situations can be awkward for the adoptive parents. This depends on the degree of communication about the adoption over the years. As long as it has not been a secret, it seems to flow fairly well for the adoptive parents. They anticipate this day happening from the early moments of adoption. However, love is never lost when given to another, and adoptive parents are always recognized as the guardians they have been to the adopted child.

FAMILY

When I wrote this book, I thought of my parents. What would they say about it? At first, I thought I was writing to complete my journey with them. Then, I realized it was not about them, just like it was not about me. Although much of the information and the lessons were about my parents, my lineage, and my history, they have turned out to be just a small part of who I am today, and the responsibility I have to take for what I am creating in this life.

Although there is no doubt that my parents and family played significant roles in my development, I am empowered to look at and to deal with my family history, let it go, and move on. I create what I want to experience tomorrow with my thoughts, intentions, and actions today. And, one of my jobs as a healer is to show others how to create their own experience.

Some important questions in Spirituality and personal growth are, "Who am I? Where am I? Why am I here? Am I present?" When you have the answer to these questions, you can determine where you want to go. You need to know the answers to these questions before you can go forward.

We choose our family on the Spiritual plane so we can learn the answers to these questions and get valuable life lessons. It may take a while to unravel what our families really are to us, and to truly understand the teachings they bring. Perspective is an elusive thing with family—we cannot see the forest for the trees.

I believe in karma and past lives. I believe I have more karmic debt or life lessons in the area of relationships and family than in other areas. The lessons have been difficult and intense in this lifetime, and I know I have not yet mastered them. When I examine the patterns in my life around relationships, I am aware of having fears of being hurt, abandoned, controlled, underappreciated, lied to, deceived, and abused. I think about these things and truly know that they are not real. They are illusions created through feelings of fear, separation, and some of the early pivotal moments in my life, such as losing my younger brother. I now see that I am never alone. Only I can hurt, abandon, control, underappreciate, lie to, deceive, and abuse myself. Only I can give that power to another. No one can do those things to me unless I let them, unless I choose for those things to be my experience. With this reality I am able to let all my hurts, abuses, and abusers go. I can forgive myself for drawing in these experiences if they caused me pain, and I can accept the lessons. None of them killed me, and they certainly have made me the man I am today. As I work with this reality, I find myself living a more peaceful life.

Without question, my most difficult relationship has been with my father. As much as he wanted to love me and as much as I love him, there was always tension between us. We have been more accepting of each other now that I am a father.

Nevertheless, this is a karmic relationship, a strong connection with a lot of polarity. We are pulled by tremendous feelings and insights that we have been here before with each other. Of course, my father had a similar relationship with his father, and my grandfather with his father; it is a clear chain in our family.

You may ask why I have not healed this relationship. I watched the pattern all my life between my dad and granddad. I encouraged them to love each other more. In my twenties, I began to try to communicate with my dad about us becoming friends. At times I was frustrated and pushed too hard. Occasionally, things would open up, and I would see what a good man he is. Other times, he shut me out and said nothing. In recent times, I have just let go and accepted him for who he is and who he is not. I have to leave the karma in that relationship and be sure to not carry it over to other relationships; otherwise, I will just recreate more karma to ensure that I get the lessons. As I continue to bring awareness to my communication with Dad, I see that old patterns and family history can be slowly shifted and healed. Ultimately, that is what I am committed to, no matter how long it takes, because as long as I hesitate to love fully, especially in a primary relationship with my dad, I will carry that with me everywhere. Somewhere in recent times I seem to have accepted myself more. I feel karma completing itself within me. The need to prove myself has lessened in recent days. It could be a sign of getting older, and it could be a sign of healing deep within the core of my being. It feels good.

This book has helped me clear a lot of karma within myself. The writing of it has taught me so much more about who I am and what I want to experience in life. It has helped me become clearer so that I can communicate this information to others. In addition, I have decided that with the best of my human ability, I will create the healthiest relationship with my family as possible. That applies to existing family and new family that is being created now.

THE FAMILY EXERCISE

Take a moment to reflect about your family and what they mirror to you about life. Use this book to deal with your family karma, and other issues. If you care to review, take a look at the first part of the book again. Examine why you chose this family and the pivotal life moments they have provided you. Is there anything with them in the Personal Journey chapter that you can release? Are you ready to move up any levels in the Pyramid of Life?

I will continue to hold a space for you to heal and to spread "the power of love" around the world as a web of light.

ACKNOWLEDGEMENTS

I give credit to my parents for all they have contributed to getting me where I am today. And, I acknowledge the teachers and guides who helped me along the path. Finally, I must recognize my biggest teacher, my daughter Ruby.

Even if you think your family knows how much you appreciate them, acknowledge their value. Write it out, even if your parents are gone. Do it for yourself. Recognize all of your helpers along the way. Gratitude is a powerful tool.

To Dad...

I want to thank you for being my dad. I do love you. I see so much of you in me, and me in you. I am sorry that I did not return to the farm to take your place, for I appreciate farm life more and more as I get older; it is a wonderful lifestyle. I learned great work habits from my childhood and for these, I am grateful. You always provided a roof over my head and food on the table, and as role models, you and Mom were consistent and stable. This taught me how to be respectful of others and myself, and for that I am grateful.

I learned that if I work, I will have money. I am not afraid to work and I am thankful for that. I learned about honesty, and about nature and how to trust it and work with it. Nature continues to be a big part of my life.

Watching our farm start at a few acres and over time grow to many hundreds of acres taught me what determination could produce. You were good at the business side of farming; many farmers were not. This helped me understand how to be a businessman. I learned that when certain pieces of equipment were unavailable, you could make them—you can do a lot with scrap metal and a welder. I learned to be creative and to trust the feminine side of myself. It is all good. I now know the joys of a good day's work. For all of this I thank you, and I love you.

To Mom...

You always fed me nourishing, good food. I was never hungry unless liver or kraut and wieners were served—I never liked those dinners. I always had clean clothes to wear and a spotless house to come home to (unless I got it dirty, which I was good at). Thank you for being patient with me.

You were a great nurse, caring for me when I was sick. I felt I was one of the luckiest boys in school because I had such a good mom.

You always scraped together a few dollars when I needed money, and you were a good go-between for dad and I. You played the buffer more than you preferred. You always cared for me and for that I am grateful.

I learned about patience from you. You were a good friend, a great mom, and I am very grateful for you. I love you.

To Julie...

I want to thank you from the top of my heart for all of your love and support. You are a pillar of strength helping me move this work forward into the world. You epitomize the word "nurturing," and I am proud to be your brother. I love you.

Recognizing the Teachers

I want to acknowledge the teachers who have helped me on the path, to acknowledge their contribution to my life and to this book. I have learned a lot from many people and from wonderful ideas, old and new, ideas put together in new formats or languages to adjust to the consciousness of the people of the new millennium. I willingly pass this information on for all to use and benefit. As I requested in the introduction, please use this information with respect and responsibility.

Teachers I readily acknowledge are Robert and Pat Elliott, James and Patricia Elliott, Hervey and Tillie Toon, Janice, Julie, Chris, and Jeffrey Elliott, Morgan Lawley, Ruby Louise Elliott, Jeremiah Comey, Tim Heath, Michael Sutton, and Adnan Sarhan, just to name a few. Know that all of these people have in some way been a big help to this book. And I give special acknowledgement to Geoff Fairbanks and Kathy Greathouse for helping me get this book written and edited. I am grateful for the guidance, dedication, and hard work of Simon Warwick-Smith, Cierra Trenery, and Karen Misuraca in helping me to publish this book. And all of my friends and family who read through the rough drafts and contributed their love and attention. Especially K. Marie, Howard, Kimberly, Jennifer, Rob and Nisha. I thank you.

Masters and teachers beyond the physical realm that have inspired and helped produce this book include God, Jesus Christ, Allah, Archangels Michael, Uriel, Gabriel, and Raphael; Joseph, Mary, John the Baptist, Ezekiel, the plant and animal kingdom (elves and fairies), hawks and hummingbirds, the elementals and the elements (earth, air, fire, and water). To all the masters, teachers, guides, and contributors to the Light of which I am aware, or unaware, I thank you.

My intention is to include all of you by holding the space for you to communicate and teach through me. Life is good and I humbly sink to my knees to acknowledge those of greater wisdom, eloquence, and courage. I pray that I am able to offer respect to all who have preceded me on this journey and the reporting of it.

The last acknowledgement goes to my daughter, Ruby. My book about healing deserves one letter to her that is full of love and admiration:

Father's Day, 2002
Dear Ruby,

You are almost six months old and one of the brightest, most beautiful things in my life. You are full of so much love, joy, curiosity, emotion, and life, that I marvel at you. I think of you and literally see hummingbirds right outside my window. Love, excitement, compassion, and patience are all the things I have better understanding of because of you.

I hear you talking to your mother and it warms my heart. Even though they are baby words, they speak volumes. Already you have a passion for expression and communication. I will do everything within my power to keep it that way for you. You have a right to be heard and what you have to say is valuable.

Big blue eyes take on a whole new meaning when I look at you. They represent the sky to me, expansive, huge, and beautiful! People stop in their tracks to look at you, they want to touch and hold you. Your soul is present in those eyes. Many have described this feeling as "an old soul." Whatever that means to you, I can tell you that you have an effect on people the moment they see you. They feel your heart and see the purity there.

You are free to choose your path and I will be there to assist when you need help. I believe you will have many opportunities to lead and help others, if that interests you.

I believe in destiny. One thing I know for sure is that it is your destiny to have an interesting life. It may take many turns and you will be offered many opportunities. Doors will open. The ones you step through are your decision. You have an incredibly creative mother who loves you more than anything in the world. She and I are both are dedicated to you. You may or may not be our only child. If you do have a sister or brother, they will be just as unique as you, yet will never replace how we feel about you. You were our first and have brought us so much. Thank you, Ruby. I am grateful for your presence and your love.

On Monday, your two bottom teeth started coming in. You have been chewing on things for months, so we thought your teeth were coming a long time ago. And you were not fussy, either!

On Tuesday, your mom started giving you mashed bananas, which you did not like at first; you spit out more than you swallowed, but now you love them.

Today is Father's Day, and now I understand what that day is all about. And, I am the proudest dad there ever was. It feels great to be your dad. You will always be my daughter, and forever my friend. Just know that love is a bond we share, and I will stand beside you through thick and thin. Live life to the fullest and there will never be a doubt. You are loved.

Appendix I

Level 1 Healer Training

In the Level 1 Healer Training class, my intention is:

- To reveal your gifts as a healer

- To solidify your confidence in those gifts through the use of tools and practical experience doing the healing work

- To increase your ability to see, hear, feel and intuit the truth

My goal will be to have you doing healing work on others, or be willing to do healing work on others by the end of the program. Based on prior classes, I know this will happen.

The training program provides you with time to work and develop as the course progresses. I find that students interested in doing healing work professionally will seriously apply themselves to the assignments and homework. The students who are doing the work for themselves and are not really sure if they can help others, will do much less outside of the class. That is okay. The universe will dictate what a person ends up doing. Exposure to the information is what is necessary. The timetable is up to God.

When you have completed Level 1, you will be able to do the work. You will have tailored your technique to your strengths, using abilities in which you already have confidence. This works well. After the training, it is important to keep doing the work to develop. A few months later, I offer a Level 2 class for the professional and for those students who are doing the work.

The following is a sample itinerary of a Level 1 class which is usually two weekends long, or a total of four days. There is a break of two weeks to a month between the first and second weekend.

Day 1

• Opening the Work: Initiation for Healer Training

• What is a healer?

• Working with a partner—each breathe for 10 minutes

• Dealing with doubt

• Intuition exercises—sensing others, reading thoughts

• Create a list of 5 to 10 people to work on during the training

• Clarity about what the work is going to do for you

• Clarity about what the work is going to do for others

• Class demonstration of a session

• Discussion of the work and the tools I use

• Energy Exercises:

  Gathering information about yourself
  Applying this information to others
  Working with the chakras

• Close the Work

Day 2

- Open the Work: developing your own style

- Weaving your training and gifts into your technique, such as massage, yoga, art, singing, or acting

- Define your gifts as a human being, how they can work for you as a healer

- Perceive others' gifts; write down a gift you see in each student

- How to hone your intuition

- Identifying and clearing blocks

- Partner work: each breathe for 20 minutes

- Discuss the clearing, grounding the work

- How to develop your own style

- Nature as a guide

- Opening to all of your guides

- Meditation: invoking your technique (gifts, guidance, intuition, Spirit)

- Discussion about the work

- Discussion about Part 2

- Assignments and communication

- Close the work

Part 1 Assignment

- Breathing 5 to 10 minutes daily

- Working with at least two people per week with the breath; each person should breathe 10 to 15 minutes

- Collecting your medicine and healing tools, including feathers, rocks, oils and techniques

- Writing about your gifts, guides, connections, and synchronicities that occur during this time

- Close the work

HEALER TRAINING LEVEL 1: PART 2 (TWO TO FOUR WEEKS LATER)

Day 3

- Open the work: discussing your technique

- How is it going?

- Trusting yourself

- Overcoming fear of touching

- Taking the work further on a personal level and with others

- How to anchor intention into the work

- Accelerating your growth

- Discussion of my technique, including preparation, intuition, trust, clairaudience, clairvoyance,clairsentient, and leaving space for God to work

- Partner work; discuss your experience to date (10 minutes each)

- Entity/energy release work

- Phone sessions

- Partner work; healing session, each breathe 25 minutes

- Discussion of session

- Close the work

Day 4

- Open the work: completing Level 1 training

- Ethics and integrity

- Partner energy exercises:

- Questions and answers about your clarity with partner

- Couples work demonstration
  Clearing energy

- Training review
  Completion
  Clarity

- Preparation for initiation
  Wash
  Smudge

- Set intention

- Initiation

- Close the Level 1 work

HEALER TRAINING: LEVEL 2

My intention is:

- To prepare you for a profession as a healer

- Deal with worth, self-esteem, and financial issues about you and your work

- Fine-tune your intuitive skills around your technique

Each student will work on a designated person or me before this class takes place so we will be able to discuss areas you need to strengthen, if applicable.

Day 1: Technique

- Open the work: technique and intuitive skills

- Fine-tune the areas you need to strengthen

- Close the work

Day 2: Financial

- Open the work: confronting your worth

- Can I call myself a healer?

- What should I charge?

  Have people been paying you?
  Is it what you are worth?

- What are your financial goals as a healer?

- Is the money from the healing work your sole income or supplemental income?

  What are your financial goals for your life?
  What is the purpose for the money you will manifest?
  What is money's purpose in your life beyond survival?

Is it tied into your overall Spiritual purpose?
How does it all fit together?

+ How I manifest

Techniques that work for me around money, worth, value, and self-esteem

+ Close the Level 2 work

HEALER TRAINING: LEVEL 3

This one-day course is for healers that are doing the work and have proven they have the desire and aptitude to lead groups. The focus at this level is an initiation to lead the group circle work. Group work is based on circle dynamics—energy moves easily in a circle. This training facilitates an opening in the healer to trust Spirit to guide his or her intuition in group work.

APPENDIX 2

HEALING KITS

The following Healing Kits are available from my website www.thereluctanthealer.com. These kits contain the basic elements for the healing work. Any of these will enhance your ability to develop your technique for healing yourself and others.

- Abundance Kit for creating abundance

- Relaxation Kit to relax and mellow out the stressed individual

- Sleep Kit to encourage a restful night's sleep

- Grounding Kit to simplify the grounding process

- Purification Kit to purify and cleanse your life and surroundings

- Spiritual Gardening Kit to help you build a Spiritual garden

- Bath Therapy Kit to relax your mind, body and soul

These products may be ordered individually to restock or add to your Healing Kit. Many of these products may be acquired elsewhere, while the following supplies are available on my website, and are guaranteed to fit my quality standards.

- Turkey feathers for smudging

- Abalone shell to hold sage

- Bag of white sage

- Sweet grass

- Cedar

- Pau Santo wood

- Sprays: Cleanse, Manifestation, Lavender, and Frankincense

- Ocean stones

- Crystals

- Didgeridoos

- Eye pillows

- Essential oils

- Healing Kit CDs

GLOSSARY

Rather than make assumptions about what you know about healing and healing terms, I will define several words I use often in the text of this book. Look over these words and see if you are familiar with them and the way that I use them. It will make your journey with me a little smoother.

Affirmation - An assertion of truth.

An assertion of truth - A positive statement that asserts what is really happening.

Chakra - Eastern philosophy term for the energy centers inside and outside the body. It correlates to the primary ductless glands inside the body. They release endorphins, which open the body. The seven primary centers are hypothalamus (brain), pineal (third eye), thyroid (throat), thymus (heart), adrenal/pancreas (kidney/stomach), ovaries/testes (pelvis), and sacrum (base of spine).

Clairaudience - Intuitive hearing and speaking, also called "the gift of prophecy"; associated with the throat chakra.

Clairsentience - Intuitive feeling also called "the gift of knowing." Associated with the heart chakra.

Clairvoyance - Intuitive seeing also called "the gift of vision." Associated with the third eye/brow chakra.

Cleanse - To free from something unwanted; also a nutritional approach to cleaning the body.

Connect - When things align and people are able to have an exchange of energy.

Dark energies - Forces from the negative-side or shadow-side that cause you to experience fear and pain.

Energy - Electrical or vibration sensations that flow through the body. They can vary from soft, ticklish sensations to strong pulsating vibrations that feel electrical. Energy can also be the combination of vitality, life force, personality, attitude, and intention.

Faith - Belief or trust in something without logical proof.

Gift - A talent or skill that somebody is born with.

Healer - A person who holds space so healing can occur.

Higher self - The God in you. The thing you connect to that lifts you.

Intention - Something that you plan to do. The state of having a purpose in mind.

Kundalini - Eastern term for the energy that moves like a serpent or ball of fire up the spine.

Light - 1. A source of illumination. 2. The energy producing a sensation of brightness that makes sight possible.

Love - A feeling of tender affection and compassion that lifts one up.

Nature - The collective forces and processes that control the phenomena of the physical world, independent of human volition. Mother Nature.

Predator - An energy, person, or group that takes from others, or destroys others for gain.

Releasing - To let go or set free something that was contained or held.

Resistance - When energy is stuck, blocked or controlled by negative emotions or forces – mainly fear.

Sexual abuse - When sexual energy is used to take from a victim their clarity, energy, and control of their bodies.

Sexuality - The connection to, and expression of, your life force. It can involve sexual appeal, or interest in sexual activity.

Soul - The eternal part of our being that is the accumulation of our Spirit.

Spirit -The energy beyond our physical known universe. It can be felt in a very electrical "goose bumpy" way in the body.

Spiritual purpose - What you are here to do. The work you agreed to do on earth in the Spirit world.

Staying clear - Freedom from anything that darkens or obscures; when you're certain and experience no ambiguity.

Truth - 1. Correspondence to fact or reality. 2. Honesty.

Universal interpreter - A leader who speaks the language of love from the heart. They stand for love and peace.

"Close the Work"

NOTES

NOTES

NOTES

NOTES

NOTES

NOTES

NOTES

NOTES

NOTES

NOTES